Reflections
on
Parenting

Reflections on Parenting

Carol Garhart Mooney

The New England Association for the Education of Young Children

BOSTON

Cover design and artwork by Emily Osman
Composition by Susan Murray-Campbell
Printing by Thomson-Shore, Inc., Dexter, Michigan

Contents

Preface

Reflections on Parenting was originally written as a series of columns for a regional family newspaper. It will have resonance for any adult who interacts with children on a regular basis, having been designed not only for parents, but for teachers and administrators to use in their work with parents.

In this collection of columns, Carol Garhart Mooney shares with us the insight of her rich personal and professional experience. Her special gift is her ability to reflect on incidents from her own life with children in such a way that we immediately recognize our own experience. The author helps us see everyday things, both large and small, from a child's point of view; by revealing to us the rationale behind the child's behavior, she helps the reader to interpret and clarify the child's perceptions, his concrete view of the world, and the special logic of childhood.

Mooney provides us with wonderful, and sometimes painful, reminders of the blind spots that adults often have in trying to raise and educate children. Yet by reflecting on her own missteps as a parent, she gives us faith that we can all make a positive difference in the lives of children.

Carol Garhart Mooney has a master's degree in early childhood education, and has taught at the preschool through college levels. She has been a preschool director and was the Child Care Coordinator for the state of New Hampshire for two years. For many years she has been a faculty member at the College for Lifelong Learning at the University of New Hampshire and of the New Hampshire Technical Institute. Mooney is the recipient of numerous awards for both her teaching and writing, including the Distinguished Faculty Award at the College for Lifelong Learning, New Hampshire Early Educator of the Year, and the New Hampshire Press Woman's Award for family pages writing. From Mooney's own point of view, however, of equal importance to any of these professional credentials is her experience as the mother of four children. The stories of and reflections on that experience bring depth and authenticity to this volume.

The Publications Committee of the New England Association for the Education of Young Children is pleased to bring you this collection. We encourage teachers to photocopy pertinent sections of *Reflections on Parenting* to send home to parents, either as individual need arises, or as part of a newsletter. Please remember to credit the author and publisher.

Edgar Klugman
Temple Fawcett
Clyde Jones
The New England Association for the Education of Young Children
Publications Committee

Introduction

Psychologist John Gray has said that women talk to make sense of what they are thinking. It's more complicated than that, of course. But perhaps that's why it's so easy to get a group of women discussing labor and delivery stories, or how and when their children began independent toileting, or reading, or driving!

Parenthood is an experience that shakes the very core of our existence. It is almost always more worrisome and more wonderful than we'd expected. There are so many things to think about; there is so much at stake. Humorist Erma Bombeck once wrote a poignant column on motherhood that described the annoying way mothers have of continuing to "mother" long after the need for it has passed; she somewhat justified the behavior on the grounds that most women find that no experience before or since their active years of parenting has brought them as close to the meaning of human existence. Renowned pediatrician T. Berry Brazelton claims that when he welcomes questions after a lecture, he is always in awe of the relief parents express at discovering that they are not alone in their struggles with children.

Reflections on Parenting recounts the experiences of one woman. Although information which might be helpful to other parents facing similar frustrations or joys is occasionally woven throughout, these stories are not intended as advice, or as a how-to on raising children. They are intended for quick reading on the subway, or in the bathtub, or while the P.E. teacher has your class of third-graders. Most of these vignettes were originally published in the family pages of a community newspaper. Readers of the award-winning column often wrote: "It made me laugh," "It made me cry," "It made me feel supported as a parent." It is in this spirit that the writer shares these anecdotes once again, as neighbors would share them over coffee, or co-workers would swap family vacation stories in the staffroom. It is also true that the writer, an early educator and mother of four children, wrote them in the style of talking out loud, to make sense of what she was thinking as a parent.

Carol Garhart Mooney
Deerfield, New Hampshire
Summer 1995

Acknowledgments

With most projects, there are many people who have helped to turn an idea into reality. My sincere thanks and appreciation are extended to all who have worked on this book.

To Tessa McDonnell for suggesting the idea. To Ed Klugman, Temple Fawcett, and Clyde Jones, all of the New England Association for the Education of Young Children, for their support and patience. To Jeannette Stone for reading, editing, and encouraging. To Marguerite Shanelaris for hours spent at the computer, honest feedback, and support! To Margaret Copeland and Joanne Parise, who force me to write when I'm not in the mood.

Most of all, to my family—David, Sean, Johann, Brian, Tom, and Erin, who have lived the stories and were willing to share them.

1

Families
in a New Age

The Logic of Families Is Irrational

Actor Peter Falk, in a film about family life, plays a devoted grandfather who is, at times, in heated discussion with his own son over approaches taken with his grandson. I am particularly partial to a scene in which the young father says, "Dad, that's not even rational."

Falk responds emphatically, slamming his fist on the table. "Son—family and rationality got nothing to do with each other!"

There are many times when most of us would agree with him. The most logical professors of logic are reduced to impassioned and illogical approaches when it comes to family. Defense attorneys and mathematicians find no defense against or solutions to tired toddlers wailing in public. The term "dysfunctional family" is too often in the press and other media, reminding us of shortcomings we already feel all too painfully.

Families could use support. I admit to chuckling the first time I heard a friend say her family puts the "fun" in the word "dysfunctional," but I agree with Jean Illsley Clarke, who wrote in *Growing Up Again* that "uneven parenting" is a much more appropriate way to describe less-than-ideal family life. Families function. Sometimes they function poorly; sometimes they function well. "Less-than-ideal family life" probably describes every family in every era. There are stresses today for American families unheard of in previous generations. What we need to remember is that there were also stresses for families in previous generations unheard of to families today. It has never been easy to make marriages work; to raise children; to balance the needs of family, work, and community life. But it has always been well worth our energy, emotional investment, and stress. Family life is an awe-inducing experience.

As we approach the twenty-first century in an atmosphere in which rhetoric on family exists everywhere and supportive policies are practically nonexistent, it is important for families to support each other. There are lots of ways to do this. It can be as easy as commenting to the parent of a wailing toddler in the check-out line at the grocery store that it sounds like someone is tired. It can be as courageous as admitting to parents struggling with teenagers that your kids came home with the police at the same age for shooting paintballs at a teacher's house...and now your delinquent is married, the father of two, and a Den Leader!

Generation after generation, we enthusiastically embrace marriage and family life. We optimistically believe we will not encounter the struggles so apparent in other people's families. This is not logical, of course. But as Peter Falk so eloquently expressed in the movie, "Family and rationality got nothing to do with each other!"

Digesting the Norms

When I asked my daughter what it was that made a family a family, I was pleased with her answer. She said, "It's when people love each other, encourage you, help you, and try not to fight."

At the same age, I probably would have responded, "A mother, a father, and children." But it's the 1990s. Times have changed. The way we view families has changed. Our experience of family is different. Just as I inferred the notion that a family was a mother, a father, and children from what I observed in my world, the books I read, the movies I saw, and what teachers and other children said at school, so has my daughter.

I'm not sure I thought of it as teaching when, in the early seventies, I started saying, "Be sure to take the newsletter home to the grownups at your house." It's just that one of the children in my class had newly divorced parents and another lived with his grandfather. I didn't want anyone to feel left out. Now we say these things without even thinking.

When my daughter was in preschool in the early nineties, norms for the family group no longer existed. As with all social change, we've struggled with the language. For a while we referred to stepfamilies, blended families, second families, and reconstituted families. It was probably our human resistance to change that compelled us to define it with these adjectives. Children today don't seem to need them.

For my daughter it's been easier. In preschool, Jennifer asked Heather why she had two moms. "My Mom's a lesbian," Heather replied.

"What's that mean?" Jen pursued. Heather gave Jen that look that only four-year-olds exchange.

"It means she lives with Janet, not my Dad, of course," Heather said, somewhat exasperated by Jen's ignorance. My daughter ate her sandwich, listening and learning. Lunch was a time for digesting egg salad and new ideas about family life.

At the child care center my daughter attended, we read books like *The Not So Wicked Stepmother* and *Two Houses to Live In*. Families were always welcome, so the children knew each other's families. Sometimes Timmy's mom and spouse picked him up; other days, Dad or Kim. We became each other's extended family. Children were puzzled by my daughter's three grown brothers. "You have the most daddies of anyone in this school!" I overheard her friend exclaim one afternoon.

A few weeks after the lunchtime discussion of Heather's two mothers, I observed a fine example of children constructing their own knowledge. A prospective parent was touring the school with his child. Most often, mothers and children visited the program, so the children were quite interested in this man and his son. "Is his mom at work?" one child asked.

"Tony doesn't know his mom," our guest stated frankly. "He has two dads instead."

The child looked puzzled. "I never heard of that," he said.

Jen was standing nearby. She placed her hands on her hips and looked Josh right in the eye. "Don't you know anything, Josh?" she said, impatiently. "It's like Heather's mom—his dad's a lesbian." Our guest looked astonished, then amused. He immediately requested enrollment papers. He'd found the right fit for his family. The children here were still learning, but among their primary lessons was that there are all kinds of families.

It's like my daughter said when I asked for her help on this piece. "Talk to me about family," I said.

"Our family?" she asked.

"No—just families, in general," I said.

"Look, Mom," she said earnestly, "I like to help you with your work. But it's not that easy. Before you write about family, you have to ask yourself, 'Whose?'"

What's in a Clothespin?

On my way to a meeting I passed a small, tidy ranch home with a fenced-in lawn. In the backyard, a young woman hung laundry on a clothesline as a small boy dug in his sandbox nearby. I took my foot off the gas pedal. I stared at this domestic scene in the way cars slow, almost involuntarily, to stare at an accident along the road. The clothesline was hexagonal and spun around the way my mother's did in the early fifties, when she hung clothes while my brother dug in *his* sandbox nearby. The day was warm for early spring, and bright sunshine flooded this yard, triggering floods of memories. I could smell the Oxydol and see the brightly colored spiral the box boasted. I remembered the early spring sights and sounds of my childhood, then puzzled over this intense moment of flashback. It occurred to me that I was drawn to the scene not so much by my own memories but by the realization that it is one not so familiar to the American landscape of the nineties.

When traveling, I frequently see pristine neighborhoods with lovely homes, but rarely see people about. They are, like many of us, away from home all day, working so they can afford to live there nights and weekends. One often sees well-designed climbing structures and play yards behind suburban homes, but rarely anyone playing there. In urban settings, where children under five used to fill the streets, stooping over ants in the sidewalk or looking in shop windows with Grandma or Dad, we now see mostly adults hurrying from one task to the next. Children are not so much in evidence, until one passes on the highway a stretch van lettered TINY TOTS or WEE CARE, with small passengers on their way back to child care after an outing to a park or zoo.

One has only to listen to the news, track the statistics, or, most accurately, talk to one of many child care providers to determine the quality of life for children who spend ten to twelve hours a day away from homes and neighborhoods. Statistics vary, but most admit that only one of every eight or ten child care settings adequately meets the needs of young children. Harvard's Juliet Schor, in her book *The Overworked American*, describes the ways that business and industry make it difficult for parents to meet both work and family responsibilities. In *Children First*, Penelope Leach outlines the steps governments must take if families are to be healthy as we enter the next century. Dr. David Elkind points out the ways that women's needs have been better met in the last two decades, while children's needs have fallen behind. Like Schor and Leach, he asserts that we could turn many of these social problems around if the public decided to do so. There is general consensus on the basic problems of our society and much research on their most likely solutions. But without political action, families will fall farther behind. As was so well stated in UNICEF's 1995 publication *The State of the World's Children*, "Unless investment in children is made, all of Humanity's most fundamental long term problems will remain fundamental long term problems."

My nostalgia at viewing a mother hanging clothes to dry while her child plays is typical of busy working moms who long for an easier way of life. The fifties are often painted as a time of domestic tranquility—a golden age for children who roamed safer neighborhoods and city streets. In *Ties That Stress*, David Elkind raises the point that tranquilizer use on the part of American females during that golden era leads us to believe the whole story was not being told.

I remember a time in a preschool room when a child asked for "one of those clips" to put his paper on the easel.

"Oh, a clothespin," I said.

The child looked at me pensively. "Whydja call it that?" he asked in earnest. It launched a discussion of how people used to hang the clothes out to dry when I was little. My brief history lesson was met with a yawn and, "You should've just put them in the dryer!" I couldn't help but be amused by the youngster's surprise that someone would spend so much time doing something a machine could do quickly and easily.

But the question we need to ask ourselves as we approach the next century is, "Are we using technology to enhance the quality of life?" For children, books on tape do not provide the same experience as sitting on the lap of a caring adult while stories are read. I would hate to think that sometime in the twenty-first century a teacher will describe uses for a rocking chair and a youngster will respond, "Why would you read when you can plug in a cassette?"

The Nineties Woman: Doing It All

The day Jan put her calendar and the day's working papers in the mailbox with her Sears bill, she knew it had gone too far. The postmaster looked at her patiently as she explained that her mind had been elsewhere when she tossed it all into the mailbox on Front Street. Grudgingly, he sent someone to retrieve her book and papers—but I know he didn't understand.

I know because my friend Pam's spouse didn't understand, either, when she threw a melting ice cream cone at a window that she thought was open when it wasn't! She'd scheduled no appointments for the day so she could take her children to the beach. By midafternoon their quality time was lacking quality, so she piled her tired youngsters into the car and went through the McDonald's drive-up window for ice cream. Sometimes busy women expect too much from a day off with their children. Pam was feeling disappointed as her youngest shrieked that the ice cream was melting on his fingers and her twelve-year-old was reprimanding her with, "Really, Mom, what did you expect? You know he always does this with a cone. You should have given him cookies."

Pam extended her hand toward the backseat and said, "Just give it to me!" It was one of those moments of parental exasperation at its worst. So she chucked the cone with more force than usual at the window she thought was open.

When her husband assessed the damage, he kept muttering in disbelief, "I'm not sure how you couldn't notice that the window was closed."

I understand that a woman, rushed by her lifestyle and listening to overtired children fussing at each other, could easily forget that a window was up and not down. I understand because I've been there. I remember a day when I went to work twice.

I didn't mean to. It just happened. My child care provider arrived at my home a little late. I had to walk my son into his second-grade classroom because his sugar cube pyramid for social studies was fragile, and I also needed to stop at the junior high to deliver a musical instrument to my seventh-grader. So by the time I reached the college, I felt like I'd already worked all day.

Classes over, I drove home, mentally making task lists for the weekend: Buy valentines for Tom. Order candy delivered to my oldest son's dorm room. Send birthday gift to Grandpa. Do groceries. Get ice skates sharpened. Somewhere in there, I forgot to fill the gas tank, but as my car coasted to a stop, I knew at once that I'd forgotten to fill it up on the way to work. A kindly stranger drove

9

me to a station and back to my car with the gas can. By the time I'd returned it to the gas station, I had decided to break my no-coffee-after-lunchtime rule, so I drove to the McDonald's window I visit every morning and ordered a large black coffee. Maybe it was my fatigue, maybe it was the smell of fresh coffee; but as I got back on the highway, I returned to work instead of driving home. It wasn't until I pulled into an empty faculty parking lot that I realized I'd put in my half-hour commute in the wrong direction.

This incident haunted me as I pondered the stresses of balancing work and family life. Talking about it made me feel better. But I wasn't prepared for the pattern that developed. Every time I told the story, another mom would give me her own, admitting that at the moment of crisis, she thought she was losing her mind.

To some extent, we are. The piece we are losing is peace. Few working women can claim peace of mind. At work we worry about home; at home we worry about work...and when we look at our calendars to see what time it is, we worry about ourselves!

2

To Think as a Child

Making Sense of the Grown-up World

"It must be harder for you than for the rest of us when your kids really mess up!" a friend said to me recently. "I mean, you're supposed to know all the things to do so that your children will act right." For years, I have heard the same idea expressed in a variety of ways. The main thrust of that idea is that living with children would not be problematic if we could just get the right information out to all parents.

I am the first to agree that we badly need more education about how children grow. But I have disappointing news for those who think that finding the right book would eliminate those behavioral difficulties that drive every parent crazy from time to time. A thorough knowledge of the finest books on raising children will only help us to know what to expect and how to react when these problems arise; there is no way to prevent them from happening. Most of the things that parents find taxing and difficult are absolutely normal behavioral responses from children who are not aware, in the beginning, of socially acceptable behavior.

The things that young children do that parents call naughty or bad often make perfect sense from the child's perspective. This is what comedian Bill Cosby refers to as "brain damage." It's what Swiss psychologist Jean Piaget referred to as "how a child thinks." It is what I like to think of as plain old inexperience.

For example, we tell children to be honest. When you are four or five, it is hard to determine just what honesty is. "Tell the truth," we say, without giving an example of what "the truth" is. Children want to please us; they study us for clues. But they hear us say on the phone that we can't take part in a fundraiser because we have out-of-town company, when they know we don't have company.

They watch us pay for a magazine at the checkout counter and then pick up a real estate brochure as we're walking out—but we don't pay for that. To a child, the two items seem the same. Why must we pay for one and not the other? Why is it okay to take candy from a dish at a neighbor's house, but not from the corner store? Why is it okay to say "ear," but not "penis?" Why are you supposed to enjoy splashing in the water at the pool, but not in the water in the toilet? Why does everyone cheer when those men on TV push people down, but get upset when children do it to someone in their way?

For children, the world can be a very confusing place. We forget this as we grow. Time, experience, or often harsh punishment force us into socially accepted patterns of behavior, and we forget what it's like to have no idea what is expected. Our task as parents and teachers is to patiently help children through their frequent blunders and, ideally, to make learning experiences of them.

The most beneficial way for parents to feel more at ease with their children's social inexperience is to compare social learning to other areas of learning in the child's life. For example, we expect physical growth and development to take place in stages, and know that it often takes many years for competence to develop. When a child learns to walk, we expect her to fall down a lot at first. When a child learns to skate, ride a bike, or climb a jungle gym, we offer encouragement and assure her that, with time, her skill level will improve. When a child learns to talk, we get excited. We say, "Yes! Water," when the baby says, "Wawa." We don't scold and say, "How many times have I told you the correct pronunciation is 'water?'" We know that, in time, she will get it right, so we encourage her. When a child is learning to read, we begin with picture books and then move on to little story books—we don't expect him to read Dante the first year in school. We help with the words that are more difficult, and we let the child know that in years to come he'll be able to read every book in the library.

But then comes social learning, and we want everything to come right now. We say things like, "Don't you ever do that again!" when our child hits or bites. And, foolishly, we expect that the young child will never do it again. Why do we think only one mistake will do it with hitting or biting, when we know how long it takes to learn everything else? Or worse, we respond to the child's biting or hitting by doing the same thing to her. We can't teach a child not to hit by shouting, "Don't you ever hit," while punctuating each word with a slap. We only offer more confusion and teach lessons we don't really intend to teach.

The fact is that raising children takes time and is hard. It takes years and many blunders to finish the job, and the end product is never perfect. Realistically, we wouldn't want it to be. Most of us are wary of the adult who always has to be right, yet we frequently act as though children should always act, talk, be right.

There are no easy answers to hard questions. Helping children to understand and function in the world is a gigantic task. It feels a little easier, however, when we take it one day at a time and strive for patience as we guide children toward the end goal of living well with others.

This includes taking a long hard look at how things appear to the eye of a child. We need to spend more time remembering what it was like.

Fred Gwynne published two books years ago that point out how confusing life can be to a child. *The King Who Rained* and *The Chocolate Moose* might give you a few chuckles and also reinforce the fact that children really are inexperienced in this world of ours. You probably have similar stories of your own children.

Here is one of my favorites from the Mooney collection. When I was expecting my third child, my son Brian was five years old. One evening when I was not at home my husband, David, gave the children a simple explanation for my absence. "Mom's friends are giving her a shower tonight," he said as he made their supper.

Later, when the phone rang, David heard Brian answer in a most grown-up fashion. "Oh, no," he said, "my mother can't come to the phone. Her friends took her out to give her a bath!"

Yes, We Listen, but Do We Hear?

On a recent flight from Washington, D.C. to Newark, I viewed a human drama that reminded me of our tendency to deny the feelings of young children.

As I was about to board the plane, the flight attendant called for persons traveling with young children and then for young children who were traveling alone. A small boy approached the attendant. He kept saying, "I'm five. I'm five" (the age at which children can travel alone on major airlines), but he looked to be about three and a half years old.

"Are you looking for your parents?" the attendant asked.

"I'm five," the boy replied.

A woman finally approached and stated, "He's traveling alone." Several passengers exchanged glances and comments, questioning the child's age. But the small boy was boarded. I could hear his sobbing as I entered the plane. He was surrounded by three flight attendants, who were struggling to calm him down.

"What's your name?" one of the young men inquired.

"I don't know," the child sobbed.

"Of course you know," the flight attendant responded, smiling. "Everyone knows his name."

At this, the little boy cried louder. The crew exchanged worried glances. "Who boarded him?" one of them asked. "They had to give you a name on the kid when they put him on the plane. Somebody find out what his name is." All of this was spoken right in front of the boy.

I could make out the word "scared" from the boy's tearful sobbing. I offered to sit with the child, explaining that I had a young son. "Thank you, but it's our responsibility," the young man politely assured me.

"He's scared," I said, then took a seat across the aisle.

With this new bit of information, the flight crew began again. "Are you afraid?" one asked gently.

The boy stopped crying momentarily and nodded his head rapidly in affirmation.

"Now, that's silly," the attendant exclaimed with the best of intentions. "There's nothing to be afraid of!" The child's sobbing broke into a loud and angry cry. He covered his face with his hands, pulled his feet up onto the seat, and then kicked at the young man who was trying to help him. Exasperated, the flight attendant leaned across the aisle. "Perhaps you could just sit with him until we get in the air," he said to me.

I moved to the seat beside the child, who was still crying and saying, "Down...go down," through his tears.

"My name is Carol," I told him, "though I have been so scared before that I couldn't remember my name if you asked me."

Abruptly, the boy stopped sobbing and stared at me. "Really?" he asked, in a tone that implied disbelief.

"Sure," I said. "Sometimes when something is new to us we're so scared or confused that we can't think about anything."

"My name is Aaron," the boy began quietly. "I'm going to see Mommy in New Jersey and I don't want to be alone and she said I had to go and planes go down and they go in the water and they go down 'cause I seed it on TV...." The voice trailed off and he began to sob again.

"I've seen those crashes on TV, too," I said. "Pretty scary."

Aaron's crying quieted a little. After a long silence between us, he said, "You seed it, too?"

"Yes," I assured him, "and every time I get on a plane I'm a little scared. But then I remember all the times I've gone on planes and I've always been safe."

Aaron wiped at his tears and said, "You're too big to be scared."

"Nobody's too big to be scared, Aaron," I said. A relieved grin slowly spread across his little face. The tiny body began to relax in the seat. "Soon we'll be moving. Then you'll hear a pretty loud noise and you will feel us going up." As the plane took off, Aaron gripped the sleeve of my jacket. Almost immediately, he became drowsy and dropped off to sleep. He slept until the plane landed in Newark.

When the flight attendant checked in, he smiled at the sleeping child and said, "I guess you convinced him there was nothing to be afraid of!"

"No," I said. "I told him that everyone else was scared, too."

The flight attendant shrugged and said, "Oh, well—whatever works."

What works for children—and adults—is recognition of our feelings when we're really upset about something. We all need respect for our fears...especially in tense moments. We cannot eliminate a child's fears by recognizing them, but feeling understood and validated can ease a little of the pain. Children experience righteous fury when they share their feelings with adults and the adult response is denial.

One might think that parents don't usually go around denying their child's feelings, but focus a few moments on these very common exchanges between parents and young children:

Child: I hate the baby.
Parent: Now that's not true, honey. You love your sister.

Child: I'm not hungry.
Parent: Of course you're hungry...you had practically no lunch!

Child: I don't want to see the doctor. She hurts me.
Parent: The doctor would never hurt you.

Child: There's a monster under my bed.
Parent: That's ridiculous! Now turn off that light!

Young children are not very sophisticated verbally. They sometimes say they feel sick when they are concerned about something. They say they have monsters in their bedrooms when the real monster is an older child who has been scaring first-graders on the school bus.

A child's words are signals. We need to listen and say, "I hear you. It's okay to have those feelings." Together, then, we can figure out what they mean, where they are coming from, and what we can do about them.

Nothing but the Truth

"Okay, who took the cupcakes?" a mother queries, looking at three-year-old Jeff and four-year-old Joshua. Still licking the evidence from their fingers, the boys look up with solemn, chocolate-covered faces and state sincerely, "Not me, Mommy."

Dad looks in on eight-year-old Kevin, who is very involved in building a model. "Someone left some of my tools outside and they have rusted!" Dad shouts angrily. "You wouldn't know anything about this, would you?"

Kevin continues to concentrate on his model, but his hands are shaking as he mumbles, "Nope."

Twelve-year-old Kristen forges her mother's signature on a progress report, later changing the D to a B before bringing her report card home.

Parents are bewildered by their children's apparent dishonesty—especially when the evidence is so obvious. "It only makes it worse when you lie," we sternly state. "Why can't you at least be honest with me?" we say, truly disillusioned.

It is surprising to learn that it is frequently our own response to the truth that encourages our youngsters to be less than honest with us. There is the classic example of the two-and-a-half-year-old who, when asked how she likes her new baby sister, honestly declares, "I hate her. I wish they would take her away!" The adult response to this is usually strong enough to teach the child that her honesty is not appreciated.

Similarly, when a four- or five-year-old, urged to kiss Aunt Harriet, says, "No, her breath always smells bad," or an eight-year-old says, "I didn't do my homework because it was a stupid assignment and I'm mad at my teacher because she isn't fair," the truth is often being told, but is rejected by the shocked adult world.

If we want to teach honesty, we must be prepared to listen to bitter truths as well as to pleasant ones. If a child is to grow up honest, she must not be encouraged to lie about her feelings, be they positive, negative, or ambivalent. Yet so often we give our children the impression that their positive responses are the only ones we are ready to accept. We are impatient with "I don't know," yet it is sometimes the only honest answer. Studies of moral development clearly indicate that the young child's approach to moral dilemmas is very different from an adult's. It is closely connected to the child's intellectual growth, and as unlike adult thought processes as a four-year-old body is unlike a forty-year-old body.

So what can parents do when their children resort to lying? Initially, relax a little. Do not equate tall tales at four or even defensive lying at twelve with perjury on the witness stand in adult life. Look carefully at the situation. Have you given such a negative response to honest emotion that your child is lying to please you? What about the twelve-year-old's report card? If the response to a D is such that a child feels compelled to change the grades "illegally," perhaps the family policy on grades needs to be reevaluated.

One of the best approaches to fostering honest communication is to avoid playing the district attorney (forcing confessions or putting kids on the spot in an embarrassing way) while calling a situation as we see it. Instead of trying to trap a youngster by saying, "How did my vase get broken?" when, unknown to the child, we actually witnessed the event, say, "I'm angry that you girls broke my vase—you know you're not allowed to play catch inside." When a young child exaggerates, be playful. You might respond, "You really wish that could happen, don't you? Now let's talk about how it is in real life."

Lastly, remember that children learn behavior from watching the significant adults in their lives. There is no better way to teach our children than to live the virtues we want them to emulate. This was recently brought home to me when a visitor at our house asked, "Do you mind if I smoke?"

I went looking for an ashtray, prepared to do my pained-acceptance routine, when my son Brian came over and whispered, "Maybe this once you should just be honest, Mom. We're out of Lysol spray!"

Don't Play with Their Food

It occurred to me recently that we have been most conscientious over the years in referring to bodily processes in a natural and accurate way to our children. At our house, the navel has not been called the belly button. The greatest transgression from the correct anatomical terms has been an occasional reference to the bottom as the bum. Yet clearly we've been negligent when it comes to defining the world of food to our offspring. I was reminded of this the other day when my eight-year-old son said, "I'm supposed to remind you to get hay for Dad today."

My neighbor, hearing this, commented, "Boy, David has his mind on that garden way before the snow melts, doesn't he?"

I smiled, not sure what to say. You see, the message—understood by father, son, and myself—really meant, "Remember to get Shredded Wheat when you're at the supermarket."

Then there was the salad dressing. For years, David used bleu cheese and I used oil and vinegar. The boys liked a homemade mayonnaise-and-catsup dressing. Over and over again, the children would hear a parent say to the other, "Dinner's about ready—why don't you mix up the boys' dressing?"

Needless to say, we never guessed the impact of this on our family culture. It wasn't until one of our sons confidently ordered a salad with boys' dressing at a restaurant that we realized we should have been more clear on these things.

Once, our oldest son came home furious after dinner at a friend's house. "How could you let me do it?" he shouted angrily. "I just humiliated myself at Matt's house. Sprouts," he shouted at me, enraged. It was one of those discussions that are extremely hard to follow. "Sprouts!" he yelled again, longing to be understood.

I was thinking salad bars and my son was reliving the moment when he walked into Matt's kitchen and said, "Oh, great! Brussels balls are one of my favorite vegetables." Finally, I understood. I tried to think of how I'd have felt as my friend's sibling roared with mirth over my ignorance.

"I'm sorry, Sean," I said. "I guess I just never thought about it."

I can still remember the dignity with which he held his small body erect. He looked me straight in the eye and said, calmly but coldly, "Well, you should have thought about it. Normal people refer to those as Brussels sprouts, and from now on I will, too."

People have not always been so hard on our family's peculiarities regarding the language of food. One of the finest displays of respect to a child and his tastes I ever observed was at the old Statler Hilton Hotel in Boston, about fourteen years ago. We met relatives for brunch and had our son, who was about two, with us. A deluxe brunch was a rare treat in those, our "student," days, so we were thrilled with the selection of crêpes, omelettes, and eggs Benedict. Sean, however, was into simpler tastes. He loved his daily banana and Cheerios. He hated the tiny blackish point sometimes found at the very tip of the banana, though. He called it "the bone."

When the stately waiter returned to take our orders, he turned to the high chair and asked, "And you, young man?"

Sean, pleased to be taken so seriously, clearly stated, "I want Cheerios and a banana with no bones."

You'd think we'd have learned after all these years to be more specific about correctly referring to foods by their accurate names. But if you come to my house you're still liable to hear one of the boys refer to zucchini as one of Dad's giant cucumbers. He does grow amazing foods. It must be all that hay!

3

Common Concerns

The Beating Goes On

Ricki Lake's guest on her morning television talk show last week was advocating corporal punishment as a means of lovingly keeping a child in line. "Children want to know who's in control," he asserted, "and physical punishment administered with love is the best way to show them."

For some of us, those words present a contradiction in terms. How does one "lovingly" hit another? Yet violence against children is so accepted in American culture that most parents believe spanking to be an inevitable part of raising children. In *Behind Closed Doors: Violence In the American Family*, the authors state, "Today most parents hit their children at one time or another. Few deny it. And if not proud of it, many honestly believe the slap on the bottom is a just and necessary tool of discipline."

It is a fascinating thing that we tend to negatively view TV and movie violence, violence in our streets, and violence in our neighborhoods; yet cherish our right to keep children in line through its use. So electrically charged is this issue that Ricki had her hands full keeping members of the audience from going for each other's throats. An opponent of corporal punishment, also a guest, pointed out that the anger in the crowd was very representative of a culture where punitive discipline is honored.

Members of the audience were too busy shouting at one another to hear the statistics the guest was quoting: most imprisoned assassins had violent childhoods; parents who abuse were abused as children.

The society we live in privately (and, too frequently, publicly) accepts violence against children. American parents want to refer to spanking as discipline, not violence. But at what point does hitting become child abuse?

English psychoanalyst Alice Miller claims that we are all tempted to excuse our inappropriate responses to children because they are not extremely abusive. In her study, *For Your Own Good: Hidden Cruelty in Child Rearing*, Miller describes the ways in which the pain of our own childhood suffering remains hidden through the use of defense mechanisms. We rationalize that we owe it to our children to bring them up well, she says, and this forces us to physically punish them "for their own good."

When an adult strikes another adult, we call it assault and battery. Yet when the suggestion is raised that hitting children should be against the law, it is met with scorn by most Americans. More than 80 percent of American parents use corporal punishment against their children—in spite of the research statistics that consistently prove that spanking is not an effective tool of discipline; it does not teach children the lesson we wish for them to learn.

The next time we are tempted to spank a child with the reprimand, "This will teach you a lesson," we should think of the lessons that are actually taught when we hit a child:

- Spanking teaches that might makes right.
- Spanking teaches that the way to solve problems is through violence.
- Spanking teaches hostility and anger.

Perhaps more frightening than these messages is the fact that spanking teaches the child that external force, rather than self-discipline, will govern her behavior. Our goal as parents is to teach our children self-control. Our goal is to help them build inner controls so the motive for their behavior is based on sound conscience—not on who's watching.

Because we live in an increasingly violent society, we must seek alternative measures of discipline. We need to model maturity, sensitivity, and kindness for our children if we want them to inherit a peaceful, productive world.

To Spank or Not to Spank?

Oprah is poised, as always. The guest speaker could be any one of the nation's leading specialists on children and the family. She has just included in her opening comments the following statement: "Whenever we spank a child, we are teaching her to hate us, fear us, and avoid us. It clearly is not a desirable method of teaching children appropriate behavior." The audience is quiet, apprehensive. The cameras scan the skeptical faces of men and women, many of them veterans of the job of rearing children. They are not convinced.

The silence is broken as the host welcomes input: "The recent caning of a young American in Singapore has everyone discussing physical punishment. Does it hurt or help? We'd like to hear from you!"

The first volunteer to voice an opinion is a plump, benevolent-looking woman. "I don't mean to criticize," she begins. "But I raised six kids. I've got fourteen grandchildren. I was a Den Mother for twenty-five years, and I say, 'When you spare the rod, you spoil the child.'" At this, the audience roars with applause. The hands, many retired now from spanking bottoms, clap wildly until the host begs for silence so the speaker can proceed.

I have viewed several programs in the last few weeks addressing physical punishment of children. The audience changes, the guest speaker varies, but the issue of spanking and the impassioned group response remain the same. It fascinates me.

On mornings when my daughter hugs me on her way out to school and says, "I love you, Mommy—have a great day!" I wonder how parents can hit their children. I settle with my second cup of coffee and write articles on the joys of raising children and also on the complex and sad issue of family violence.

On rainy days, though—when one child storms out of the house, shouting, "How can you expect me to wear that ridiculous raincoat in public? I'd rather be soaked!" and another is blaming his poor English grade on our "outdated computer!"—I want to join the applause. I weaken. I'm angry. I feel like punching someone.

I am not alone. Most of us have days like this: we want to be good parents; we vow to end the spanking, the shouting, the frustration and tears. All too often, however, we fall into the same old patterns. Why? Parenthood remains a profession staffed mostly by amateurs. Many parents feel confused, guilty, and alone in this job of raising children. Many adults are not comfortable with striking a child. We rationalize the situation with statements like, "This is going

27

to hurt me more than it hurts you," or, "It's for her own good." We are afraid that if we are too permissive, our children will run wild. Permissiveness has been blamed for the rise in crime, the decline of the public school system, vandalism, drug abuse, delinquency, and most other contemporary social ills.

It would be naïve to suggest that the state of family life in America is just fine. We do have problems. However, the punitive measures suggested by those who applaud Singapore's approach are surely not the solution. Discipline and punishment are not the same thing; discipline goes beyond attempts to eliminate negative behavior and strives to teach positive behaviors instead. Spanking is not an effective tool in child discipline. Once we employ spanking or shouting, our only alternatives are spanking harder and shouting louder.

Parents often say, "I spank him and it doesn't do a bit of good!" In fact, spanking sometimes leads children to feel they've "paid" for their mistakes and are now free to make a few more. It offers no incentive to change undesirable behavior.

What, then, are the alternatives? The Princeton Center for Infancy suggests that the most important discipline techniques for parents of young children are anticipation, diversion, and substitution. In other words, if we have shopped all morning and our toddler has missed her nap, it's no time to go to the library in the hope that she can "be good" for another half-hour. If our four-year-old is distressed after supper when Mom leaves for work, the child care provider can be ready to read his favorite story or play a new game. If our ten-month-old keeps reaching for the phone on the end table, move it out of reach and substitute a play phone so baby can talk.

For older children, allowing them to experience the natural or logical consequences of their own actions can sometimes be the best approach. For example, when our sixth-grader comes home without his sweatshirt, he is angry with himself for losing it. We frequently lecture about responsibility, moralize about the cost of clothing and the value of a dollar, tell the child we'd have gotten a good stiff punishment in our day—and then replace the sweatshirt immediately. Perhaps a better approach would be to acknowledge the child's predicament while letting him deal with the problem. We could say, "You must feel angry with yourself for losing your sweatshirt. I remember how I felt when I lost my watch. It will probably be a while before we can afford to replace it." This offers the child an opportunity to learn from his actions and also to keep his dignity intact.

For parents seeking a direct route to better relationships at home, try modeling your actions with your children on your relationships with your close friends. How many of us would greet a friend's lament over a lost item of value with, "When are you going to be more responsible? I should have known you couldn't keep track of your things. It serves you right!"

In the last analysis, it is our own behavior which teaches children how to live. Therefore, nothing is more ludicrous than an angry parent shouting, "Don't you hit!" and punctuating each word with a slap. When adults hit children, we don't teach the lessons we really want to teach. Spanking truly serves no purpose in shaping a child's character. Yet, given the stresses of parental responsibilities, parents who manage eighteen years of guidance without ever slapping a hand or bottom are in the minority.

Parents can support each other in this joyful, challenging work by sharing strategies that have worked for them, recommending books or community resources which help parents through hard times, and, especially, by recognizing that the struggles we experience are common struggles. We are not alone.

Can Babies Be Spoiled?

Recently, at a social gathering where I knew almost no one, someone introduced me as a child development specialist. My arm was immediately grasped by a new grandmother who asked a question so common to discussion of infants that it surprised me that I'd never addressed it in my column. With a benign smile (and an apprehensive glance at her daughter), the older woman spoke directly. "We have been having this little disagreement about the new baby. My daughter carries her around day and night in that little thing." (She pointed to the Snugli sling, where an infant slept peacefully). "I have warned her that the baby will soon be a tyrant if she doesn't let him know who's boss right away. Maybe you can settle this for us. Can babies be spoiled?"

I stood there wishing someone would drag me away to serve crackers and cheese or to get ice. Images of spoiled things flashed through my mind—cantaloupes, fish, curdled milk—but I couldn't for the world bring up an image of a spoiled infant. Yet the kind of repugnance we feel at opening a gallon of milk gone bad can be compared to the look on this grandmother's face when she spoke of her grandchild's crying. The baby was four weeks old.

Though child development texts have stressed for years that there are both physiological and psychological reasons for infant crying, most of the conventional wisdom passed from generation to generation has focused solely on the physiological ones. "If you have checked and the baby is dry, warm, and fed...then let her cry it out!" This was clearly the stand of the grandmother I was facing. Fortunately, this limited view of infant crying has changed in recent years.

"I think it's nearly impossible to give a newborn too much attention," I offered weakly. The mother smiled. The grandmother frowned. "Excuse me, I need to make a phone call," I said, and rushed out of the room.

The incident brought back memories of the early days of my own parenting, when two grandmothers, two great-grandmothers, and one great-aunt watched every move I made. It was the belief of all these women that if the baby wasn't hungry, wet, or cold, then crying was an attempt to get undue attention—and should be nipped in the bud.

As a teacher of child development, I find that this attitude is still widely held by large numbers of the general population. It is clearly a positive move that most new parents are responding to their infants' cries despite pressure to the contrary from extended family and other unsolicited sources of help. However, many young parents admit that in the back of their minds is the nagging worry that maybe they will raise a spoiled brat by tending to their child's every tear.

There are several things we should think about when dealing with crying in infancy. First, crying is communication. Infant crying cannot be compared to persistent crying and whining on the part of a five- or six-year-old who can use words. Crying is the only language an infant has. It is a signal that there is a need to be met. Though this need is often recognized as hunger, fatigue, discomfort, or wetness, it can also indicate that an infant is frightened or lonely. When infants cry, the appropriate response of parents is to go to the baby to see what can be done to make her more comfortable.

Some babies cry very little. Some babies cry a great deal. A frequent misconception about infant crying is that the amount is in direct relation to how well the infant's needs are met. This is unfortunate, as it can make new parents feel very inadequate very quickly if their baby is one of the screamers.

It can be difficult for parents when their infant cries frequently and won't be comforted. However, this is not a plot on the part of the newborn to keep you busy. Often the condition is what is sometimes referred to as colic. When a baby has colic, she goes through a period where she cries continually and in a frenzied way for no apparent reason. No measure of feeding, cuddling, walking, talking, or rubbing the tummy seems to improve matters. The baby appears miserable and gets so tired from all the crying that sleep becomes impossible. This is the most trying of times for parents who, obviously, are losing a lot of sleep, too. These are the times when most parents admit to fleeting fantasies of violence!

Try to remember that your infant is not trying to test your patience. She is experiencing distress, and needs your love and comfort. Even if you feel your efforts make no difference because the baby continues to cry, your infant will be aware of your love and comfort. And she needs that to get through this difficult time.

Toilet Teaching: Toddler Knows Best

When my oldest child was just about two, he spent every morning perched on the side of the tub, listening to the morning news and watching his father shave. Then they would splash on aftershave and go downstairs to fix eggs. I soon reaped a benefit of all this shared bathroom time. Before his second birthday, my son posed the question, "If I stand to pee like Dad, can I get stripes on my diapers, too?"

I had not begun to introduce the idea of potty training, so I was taken aback by the question. "Well, sure, honey, when you're older you can have pants with stripes at the top and you can stand to pee," I responded, probably absent-mindedly.

"No! Now! I can reach it now. I'll pee like Dad now!" he assured me with the passion that only two-year-olds can bring to the words "no" and "now!"

Parents of toddlers can understand why I immediately responded with, "Fine! You want to stand to pee now, then we can arrange that." So off came the diaper and up to the toilet marched my young son. Of course, he couldn't really "reach," and so he urinated at the toilet, not in it. I was, nonetheless, impressed by this accomplishment. We put a small step near the toilet and bought size one BVDs with stripes at the top, and our first child was toilet trained. From that week on, he used the toilet. We never purchased a potty chair.

When I hear such stories from other parents, I am always inclined to say, "I find that really hard to believe." It doesn't often happen that way. My other children were more of the we'll-be-taking-Pampers-to-school variety.

For some reason, however, we are relaxed about differences in development in some areas, and uneasy in others. For instance, some children walk at eight months, others at ten months, and some at eighteen months. Yet none of us say, "I don't know what to do with her—she just refuses to walk!" We accept that when our child is ready, she will walk. Some children begin losing baby teeth when they're as young as four and a half; others are seven and still haven't made a claim with the tooth fairy. Yet none of us say, "I'm so embarrassed—she's six and a half and doesn't even have one loose tooth." Instead, we assure our youngster that all things come in time: if she is patient, her day for a tooth under the pillow will come.

Yet we forget our own words if we find ourselves with a three-and-a-half-year-old who isn't toilet trained or a six-year-old who isn't ready to read. We need to keep in mind that eating, eliminating, sleeping, and learning are all natural processes. They will happen without our interference. It is a poor use of our energies to let these routines develop into power struggles or confrontations.

Years ago, parents worked very hard at toilet training their babies during their first year. Today, however, we realize that the child's readiness, not the parents' effort, is the critical factor in toilet training. How do we know if a child is ready? Usually during the second year of life, children establish a fairly regular pattern of eliminating. We notice when diapering our child that she is staying drier for longer periods of time. It also becomes apparent when the toddler is having a bowel movement. She may take on a distracted look and stop what she is doing. She might look very absorbed in thought or develop a pattern of going to a particular place in the room.

These are all clues that your child is becoming aware of the process of elimination; the very first step in toilet teaching. Parents wanting to encourage the child can increase the child's awareness by stating matter-of-factly, "I see you're doing your BM." The use of such common expressions as "pooey," "stinky," "yucky," and the like can actually inhibit the process we are hoping to encourage.

Toileting behavior is an area in which we often give children the kind of mixed signals that could be confusing to anyone—but especially to a toddler, for whom the world is already a most perplexing place. It is impossible for a two-year-old to understand that the very same accomplishment that brought acceptance and approval in the potty chair can bring disapproval or anger when left on the coffee table. Therefore, it is important for parents to be matter-of-fact in this effort. Try not to overreact. Your toddler has no idea of sanitary habits.

Given the opportunity (and toddlers seem to find them!), playing with her stools is as much fun as playing with sand, water, finger paints, or any other materials. She enjoys squeezing and smearing. So it makes sense that this whole process of elimination is a most confusing one for the young child. While a harsh response is inappropriate, we must explain that BMs are for the toilet, not for playing. Children also often view their bowel movements as part of themselves; some may protest when stools are heartlessly flushed away.

For all of these reasons, it makes sense to wait on toilet teaching until your child can talk with you about the toilet and make some connection between her bodily processes and adult expectations. It's not something you can rush. Though parents hear about the One-Day Method for Toilet Training, it's likely that the children for whom it works were well on their way to being trained, anyway. A crash program is not a tremendously effective way for most of us to learn anything. If your child is two and a half years old and not trained, but the day care center won't accept her in diapers, try to find a family child care home for another six months. Let your child's development be the impetus behind toilet teaching.

There really is no best way to introduce toileting to toddlers. Different approaches work with different children. However, there are a few general things to keep in mind. Avoid battles; if children are pressured on this point, they usually react by continuing to soil their pants or by becoming badly constipated. Small children need to urinate frequently; accidents are bound to happen now and then. Every child has his or her own pattern and pace of development. By the time one reaches adulthood, the age at which one walked, lost teeth, or used the toilet for the first time have little importance. However, how one felt about those developmental landmarks will remain.

Explosive Area: Enter at Own Risk

Most parents can recall several incidents which made them want to disappear. You know the times I'm talking about. You're in a crowded elevator and your three-year-old says loudly, "Have you ever seen anyone as fat as that man?" Your grandmother comes to visit and brings a friend for tea; your ten-year-old comes in and says, "Wow—awesome! How did you get your hair all blue like that?" You're at the checkout counter at the mall and, when you pull out your MasterCard, your child says, "Are you out of money again, Mom?"

But I think the worst moment is when you're in a restaurant, supermarket, or department store and your child bursts into a full-blown temper tantrum. It is not necessary to describe in detail the kicking, redness of face, and thrashing of arms and legs that accompany these tantrums. If you have been fortunate enough to miss this in your own child, surely you've observed it—at the post office, or the market, or the library.

Parents are often relieved to discover that temper tantrums are as normal in childhood as fevers or chicken pox. Not every child has them. Some children have them frequently. Can parents do anything to prevent a child from being tantrum prone? Most experts say no. It is often an issue of temperament. Yet many parents whose children have never had tantrums say, "If that were my child I'd show her what to do with that temper!" This leaves the parents of the kickers and screamers feeling very inadequate and defensive.

Adults are quick to accept a range of temperaments and personalities in their peers. Too often, though, we have a stereotype where children are concerned. We like them to do what they are told—whether it makes sense or not. We expect them not to complain or pout. We like them to be quiet, charming, and respectful. We are horrified at children who shout, "No!" at their parents or, worse, give their parents a smack when they can't have what they want.

We forget that a two- or three-year-old knows if she's hungry for ice cream, but does not know what to do with her frustration if her request is denied. For one child, the response may be to kick or scream. For another, a pout is quite enough. Some of us shout, swear, or throw things when we're angry; others write, bake bread, or take long walks. Likewise, children have their own ways of dealing with stress or frustration. Some reaction is pure individual expression; some of it is learned.

As parents, we have the opportunity to help our child with that part of the anger response that is learned. The first step is to take a good look at how we deal with frustration ourselves. For many of us, managing our anger is not easy in adulthood. One reason for this is that we learned as children that anger is bad rather than normal. This idea persists, and we pass it on to our own children, even though we are vexed with ourselves for not better dealing with our negative feelings.

How do we break the cycle? We have to convince ourselves that it is just fine for youngsters to get very angry. Then we have to patiently help our children channel their anger in an acceptable direction. I say "patiently" because it takes a very long time for a child to learn to say, "I don't like it when you do that," rather than giving the offender a good slap. The child learns to deal with her feelings and actions by watching us. Example is the true teacher.

I've always thought it was a conspiracy against parents to pile all that candy and gum within the reach of a child at the supermarket checkout. It's normal for children who see it to want it, reach for it, and whine and cry when their parents thwart their efforts. I encourage parents of preschoolers to unite! Don't be embarrassed when your child does what any young child would do in that situation. In a quiet voice, acknowledge your child's frustration. You might say, "I understand why you are so angry—you really want some of that candy and we are not going to buy any." Don't expect your child to take this news gracefully. Pay for your purchases, giving as little attention to your child's wails (and anyone's stares!) as possible. Remember that it is reasonable to say no to the candy, but it is unreasonable to expect your child to like it. Her knowledge that you realize that her anger is justified can help the child feel better. Fortunately, more and more supermarkets are offering a candy-free checkout line. I applaud these efforts.

We have all seen how ineffective it is to say, "You stop that right now, young lady!" Each time the parent issues a command, the child screams a little louder. A power struggle is in progress. The young child, who usually has more energy than the tired parent, can always yell louder and longer. The parent feels defeated and the child learns no lesson in effectively dealing with frustration.

Many parents have confided that the only time they've ever hit their children is in response to a public tantrum. When asked why they would respond differently at home, most parents admit that in public it is not really their children's behavior, but what people are thinking, that bothers them. "I feel like everyone is saying I'm an awful parent to allow my child to have a tantrum," one mother told me, "so I act very stern in public. But at home I just let her shout it out."

Parents often fear that they are allowing their children to establish bad habits by accepting or ignoring their tantrums. Actually, giving in to unreasonable demands in order to prevent these scenes is far more damaging to the child's development. By verbally describing the child's feelings each time she is furious, sad, or disappointed, we teach her that it's okay to be angry, sad, or disappointed; that life is sometimes like that and we will try hard to help her cope.

Children must learn at an early age that it's impossible to always have whatever they want. They need to learn to cope with the bad times life offers. In order to do this, they must have supportive adults in their lives who help them to understand feelings of anger and disappointment.

It is important for parents of very young children to remember that kicking, screaming, and crying are the only tools the child has to express frustration prior to developing strong speaking skills. Our job, if we truly want to teach, is to accept our child's behavior; to understand that by our example she will learn more acceptable ways of expressing her fury as she learns to communicate with words instead of actions. If your toddler is tantrum prone, chances are this is her best way of dealing with the stresses of life. For another child, thumb-sucking or attachment to a blanket serves the same purpose. If accepted as part of the growing process, the tantrums, like the thumbsucking and blankie, are always outgrown.

In the interim, try to walk out of the room when the explosion begins—this is often the most difficult but wisest response; attention only fuels the fire of a blazing tantrum—unless the child's behavior is already so out of control she could scare herself. In this case, quietly sitting with the child or holding her firmly might be the best choice.

Try to anticipate hunger and fatigue patterns; a rested, comfortable youngster is better able to cope with the ups and downs of toddlerhood. Be sure your child's toys are age-appropriate. If you notice that he tries a puzzle or game and is furious because he can't manage it alone, put it away for a few months. Arrange the play area to maximize independence. Put toys where children can reach them easily; put away breakables during this stage. "No-no" means so much more if it is reserved for stairs or the wood stove. If everything's a no-no, your child is bound to be frustrated and the word won't mean much when it's really needed.

Dr. Stanley Turecki's book _The Difficult Child_ was published a decade ago, but still serves as an excellent resource for people whose children are tantrum prone. He offers insight and support to parents engaged in this age-old struggle between themselves and their children.

"Family Feud"—
and Other Games Siblings Play

Years ago I read a wonderful book by Kathleen and James McGinnis entitled *Parenting for Peace and Justice*. The book offered plans for helping children to deal with the violence in our culture. It raised questions on world hunger, racism, sexism, and war toys. I pulled it out recently for a refresher reading. As is often the case when I am foolish enough to look seriously involved with a book right in the middle of the family room, violent elements invaded my space.

"You broke my hockey stick, you jerk," shouts my ten-year-old, "and you're gonna pay!"

"That's right—run to Mommy, you wimp!" retorts the twelve-year-old, a little louder.

Not to be outdone, my five-year-old shouts, "Shut up! Shut up! I can't hear 'Sesame Street'!" When the older boys do not instantly respond to his demand, this fierce preschooler charges across the room, administering kicks and fists to his rowdy brothers.

"Thomas," I say, groping for patience. "I can see that you are very angry that you can't hear Big Bird, but I can't let you kick your brother. Let's go read some books together."

We leave the room with shouts of "Jerk!" "Wimp!" "Jerk!" "Wimp!" dying in the distance. I select a good book about anger, *Boy, Was I Mad* by Kathryn Hitte, to share with Thomas, and gently place *Parenting for Peace and Justice* back on the shelf for future reference. World peace seems too lofty a goal when a little bit of domestic tranquility is so hard to come by!

Sibling savagery seems to be a big complaint among parents. "Where does it come from?" we ask each other. "How can they be so hateful?" "Why is it that they watch TV or play in peace on Saturday mornings until we get up, and then mayhem breaks out?" "Why don't they do this to the sitter?"

Too often we dismiss the question, "Where does this rivalry come from?" with the overly simplified response, "It's natural: there's always competition between brothers and sisters." One of the best analogies I've heard for the intensity of these feelings of rivalry is the comparison of the birth of a sibling to the introduction of a third spouse into a marriage. Even with assurances that there is enough love to share with everyone, that "this new person does not mean I love you less," most of us have to work really hard at sharing the special people in our lives!

For children, the task is enormous. They love their parents more than anyone else in the world. They love them more than friends, grandparents, or brothers and sisters. They say to us at an early age, "I love you the mostest." They want us to love them "the mostest" back. If there are two or more children in a family, each child still wants to be loved the most. It is difficult for children to accept being one of many in their parents' lives.

Understanding this, of course, does not eliminate the bickering, but it can have an impact on the way we react. It also enlightens us as to why it is easier for the sitter, and why the children seem to "start up" whenever we walk into the room. Much of the fighting is intentionally directed at drawing parents into the argument. After all, if Dad sides with you, you can prove he loves you best!

Experts agree that this desire to be number one is at the root of most sibling rivalry. It is healthy, normal, and actually quite understandable. So what are parents to do? Refusing to be drawn into these arguments is the best and most sensible solution. It is not, however, an easy thing to do. For instance, we are afraid to let a five-year-old and a twelve-year-old battle it out. Shouldn't we protect the younger child? By interfering in children's conflicts, we are reinforcing the very behaviors we wish to eliminate. When we take sides, we are keeping the "seesaw" in motion.

Think about it. Your younger child comes in screaming. He's been brutally bullied by his big sister. You get angry and send your daughter to her room with another lecture about how cruel it is to pick on someone younger. She gives a killing look at little brother, whose sobs have already been replaced by a smug smile. Don't think big sister will let this one pass. Most children spend time in exile not repenting for their behavior, but planning their retaliation. So the process continues.

How do we break the cycle? There are several things we can do to reduce friction. We must focus on the word "reduce," and not hope to eliminate sibling rivalry. It is normal and will always be there. The following tips can actually help children to avoid conflicts.

- If it's at all possible, children in their middle years do better if they don't have to share a bedroom.
- Always bite your tongue when tempted to say, "Why can't you be more like your brother/sister?"
- Assure each child on a regular basis that she is valued for her uniqueness; that she is loved and special.
- If possible, schedule time alone with each of your children away from home. Go out to eat or take a walk together.

- When children engage in verbal or physical conflict, leave the room. If you are working in the room, ask the children to take their conflict to another room.
- Do not be drawn into arguments as a mediator. Respond pleasantly ("I'm sure you two can work this out"). Then leave the room.
- Ignore bickering whenever possible. When children are happily engaged together, stop to talk with them. Smile. Say, "You two look like you're having a good time." Research tells us that parents tend to ignore children when they are playing well together, and attend to them when they are not. This encourages conflict when children want attention.
- Don't encourage "tattling." Respond only to those situations that you have actually observed.
- So many conflicts arise over who gets the "biggest half." At our house, the person who divides the last of the ice cream, broccoli, or whatever gets last choice of the portions he measures!

When children realize their parents are no longer going to play the "seesaw" game, their motivation for misbehavior drops considerably. They learn to cooperate and work as a group. When left to their own devices, children often establish a fairness among themselves that we couldn't hope to duplicate.

When the Growing Gets Rough

My daughter Erin is a handful. My friend Jane is glad; her daughter, too, has been a handful. She says I needed this. I think Jane must not like me anymore. Nobody needs this. "It's good for you. It will bring balance to your work," Jane says with a grin.

"Except if I try to write about the joys of parenting. These days, everyone who knows me will claim I'm a fiction writer," I respond grimly. I'm having a hard time. Erin is twenty months old and still wakes up a lot at night. When we tell her it's nighttime and she must stay in bed, she sometimes throws up. She stands up in her high chair, her stroller, and the grocery cart. There is no safety belt that she can't figure out how to open. Before she was a year old, she got out of the car seat that had kept her siblings comfortably secure till age three.

When school started this fall, we decided to have a regular Sunday family breakfast. We selected family-style restaurants where you can take six people to eat, two of them teenage boys, and still be able to pay the mortgage when you're done. Places with paper placemats and lots of high chairs, where you can feel comfortable taking a toddler. But not our Erin. At one recent Sunday brunch, several other families were toting toddlers. These children sat in high chairs, delicately chewing Cheerios. Erin started banging her tray and barking like a dog.

One by one, the other toddlers joined her. It was like watching The Wave develop at a football game. The babies loved it; the parents were appalled. One young couple left half-eaten omelets and whisked their daughter out the door—not without a few cold stares in our direction and a stage-whispered, "We can't have this behavior, Kimberly, it's rude to the other diners."

If my seventeen-year-old's three entrees hadn't just been placed on the table, maybe we'd have made a quick exit. But we didn't. We tried crackers, sausage, and juice. We tried finger rhymes, read story books, and pulled engaging toys and games from the diaper bag. Finally, our fifteen-year-old finished his meals and took her to the car. So much for the family brunch idea.

At children's shops, where mothers and children, as well as lots of clothes, are on display, my daughter is a terror. If I try to see if something will fit, she kicks and wails or goes still on me. While the mothers of mild children who clutch their teddies and smile adorably look on, I try to write a check with one hand while balancing Erin on one hip as she wriggles and kicks for her freedom.

41

T. Berry Brazelton reminds us that some children are simply more full of it than others, and that parents of the wild child should psyche themselves into being as comfortable in public as parents of the mild child. Shouts of "Mine!" and "No!" are healthy signs of developing independence. "Toddlers do not understand the meaning of socially acceptable behavior."

Many adults do not have patience with the behavioral needs of toddlers. A recent case in point was the woman in a children's shop who glared at me with disapproval when my daughter clutched her bear and said, "No! Mine!" to a small girl who wanted only to say hello. "Mine. Mine. Mine," she continued to chant as I took my purchase to the register.

"When you have another, she won't act so selfish," the salesclerk said bluntly.

"I have three others," I responded, "and each of them went through this, as I recall." I couldn't help thinking she was an unlikely employee for a children's shop.

One of the benefits of spending many years working with children, or living with them, is the acquired experience that helps you realize that difficult behaviors and stages usually pass. For the parent whose first or only child is full of it, getting through these times can be especially trying.

We all tend to respond to negative feedback from others. And the fact remains that the public generally smiles benevolently on parents of quiet youngsters, and glares at parents of rambunctious children as if the parents should put a stop to this behavior at once. It is more difficult to get through the days of toddlerhood with a very active child. You are understandably more prone to fatigue, impatience, and discouragement. You are not as likely to savor each moment of this period, and sometimes wish it would pass a little more quickly. But active toddlers need support for their curiosity, exploratory behavior, and strong drive for independence.

And parents need to encourage each other when the growing gets rough. Despite a tiny bit of misery-loves-company gloating, my friend Jane has helped me to see the light at the end of the tunnel. At four, her daughter is delightful company these days.

Erin will not insist on standing up in the shopping cart forever. She will stop unrolling the toilet tissue and pulling all the Kleenex from the box. Someday she will say "yes" and "yours" instead of "no" and "mine." She will leave her shoes on, go to bed without a struggle, and stop putting her dish on her head when she's had enough spaghetti. Her tricycle will be replaced by a ten-speed, then a car. With a lump in my throat, I'll say to Jane, "They grow up too soon." But today, as I pick up the Kleenex for the third time and fish *Psychology Today* out of the toilet, I'm not begging time to stand still.

"It does get easier," Jane says with a smile. Most days I believe her.

Love That Shouldn't Be Alike

"I love you all the same!" my mother used to say whenever one of us hinted at the preferential treatment of a sibling. Now, my mother was an only child, so maybe she believed this. But having grown up with four siblings and having had four children of my own, I know better. For one thing, some of us are just easier to get along with than others. We may not be sure why this is, but if we are honest, we admit that it's true.

Current research suggests that children bring with them into this world a temperament uniquely their own. Certainly, things like parent interaction and birth order in the family affect children, also. But it would seem that some infants are born rather content, and others rather fussy. And though we all profess to love our offspring deeply, it's easier to enjoy parenthood with a content infant than it is forever trying to calm a fussy one. Thus, our parenting behavior is often a dance with our child; a reaction to his or her behavior.

When we have more than one child, we become aware over time that one is easier to talk with, another easier to work with. Perhaps still another makes us laugh easily when we are down in the dumps. The flip side to this, of course, is that one makes us cry more easily, one sparks our anger, and another sometimes acts like the brother, cousin, or aunt we could never stand. The hardest challenge, perhaps, is the child who reminds us of our own childhood difficulties, sometimes prompting us to look the other way to ease our own discomfort, just when our child needs us most.

To set, as a goal, not having preferences among our children is worthy, but achieving this goal can be tricky. We can pledge our love and commitment to all our children, but the expression of this will be made in different ways and at different times with each child.

It is comforting to me, as a parent, that experts encourage us not to try to make everything equal among our children. I've tried at times to do just that, but I could never manage it. According to Carole and Andrew Calladine, authors of *Raising Brothers and Sisters Without Raising the Roof*, doling out gifts or special times on a perfectly equal basis only encourages children to keep scrupulous tabs on who gets what when. Rather, they suggest, view each child as an only child. Take her interests, time, age, and needs into account whenever planning special times. Don't buy two tickets to a baseball game if only one child really enjoys the sport. Children are less likely to compete with each other if they know they are viewed individually.

On the other hand, reducing, not eliminating, sibling squabbles is the best we can hope for. Conflict is a normal part of all intimate relationships. Sharing a parent's love and attention is the most difficult challenge a child faces in her early years. There is bound to be some rivalry, but it can be kept to a minimum. Anne and Herman Roiphe, in *Your Child's Mind*, point out that "A happy home is not one in which no feelings of anger or spite are expressed. A happy home is not a harmonious melody: at best it is one in which the cacophony is not constant and individual voices can be heard above the din!"

Sometimes we forget, as children's fighting escalates on a rainy day, that the primary goal of children's arguing is to control us, not each other. Ignoring inconsequential bickering is often the best approach. Having ground rules—such as no brother or sister is allowed to hurt another, or bickering in front of Mom or Dad is not allowed—can be helpful. But the key ingredient remains our refusal to allow ourselves to be drawn in as arbitrators.

When a child comes whining that she's been victimized, try responding with empathy, a hug, and some form of, "You sound really angry. I hope you girls can work out a solution soon because it probably hurts both of you." What you are really saying is, "I hear you. I care about you. But this really is your problem to work out, and I'm confident that you'll manage it!"

Periodically, my children have all said they wished they were only children. They have all claimed that we always think they are the bad guy. They have all sworn that they never get the biggest half. These are always hard times for me; times when I hear my mom's voice proclaiming, "Come on, now, I love you all the same."

So I take a deep breath and say, "I love you all differently, and today it sounds like you feel it's just not enough." Someday they'll understand, I hope, that it is the best I could possibly offer.

4

Tender Topics

"Grampa
Won't Be Visiting Anymore..."

What should children be told about death? And when?

My son, a jet pilot in training, is always responding to concerns for his safety with the reminder that, statistically, I am at greater risk driving my car than he is flying a plane. Still, the number of plane crashes in recent years leaves families feeling at least slightly stressed until their relatives reach their final destinations. The grieving process is enormous for families when a loved one leaves for a routine trip and never returns. There is no time to say good-bye. The shock of such sudden death brings pain to surviving family and friends that is almost impossible to endure.

The loss is sometimes most severe for children, because of the inability of adults to share the grieving process with them. We should begin when children are young, gradually introducing them to the idea that death is part of the life cycle. But most often, the whole subject of death is avoided, consciously or not.

For children with no prior understanding of death, the sudden loss of a parent or loved one can be devastating. For many relatives of accident victims, children included, there is guilt in addition to the anguish and grief. Bereaved people have asked themselves, "Why didn't I drive him to the office?" "Why didn't she just call in sick?" "Why did we say we hated the baby-sitter?"

Elia Parsons, in *The Mother's Almanac*, advises that children be told that pain and loss are part of life. They must understand that accidental death is just that. Accidental. Bad luck. Children need the reassurance that nothing they did or didn't do could cause a tragic accident. Children already know that losing a loved one hurts. They need to know that the hurt may take a long time to go away. They need adults who will be patient, adults who will help them find appropriate outlets for their grief.

The young child is curious about everything. Death is no exception. At a funeral home two years ago, I saw two cousins, eight years old, slowly approach the kneelers before their great-grandmother's coffin. They knelt down and folded their hands as they had seen the grown-ups do. In unison they bowed their heads, mouthing what one would expect to be prayers. I, however, was close enough to hear the words.

"You do it."

"No, you!"

Quickly, both boys reached out and touched the leg of the deceased. "She's cold and hard as a log," said one.

"Yeah—a frozen log," the other replied.

Nearby, an elderly man gasped. "Well, I never! Kids today can't even respect the dead!"

It is easy to understand the offended feelings of this friend of the deceased. But it is also easy to understand how these two young boys could not resist the driving urge to find out a little more about how you feel when you're dead.

Nobody really gives them much information on the subject. When the goldfish died at school, a favorite teacher said, "Now he's gone to that great fishbowl in the sky!" He even let all the children say their good-byes before flushing the fish away. When Tommy's grandfather died, his grandmother said, "The Lord has called him to do important work." Peter wondered if God had called Tommy's grandfather on the phone for this important work, or did he just shout down from the clouds? Whether a family is religious or not, it is a poor response to a child's inquiry on death to say, "Oh, Nana has gone to God." That means nothing to a child.

For so long, we tried to shelter children from the brutal realities of terminal illness and death. But what is most brutal to children is the images they conjure up in imagination and dreams when adults avoid their frank requests for information and help. They can usually cope with the truth when it is offered in a direct way and backed up with support and reassurance. In her book *On Death and Dying*, Elizabeth Kubler Ross tells the story of a terminally ill five-year-old child who needs his parents' help desperately. "I know I'm going to die and I'm so very scared," he told the doctor, "but my parents just won't talk about it."

It is helpful to children and adults, when they are ready, to recall pleasant days and memories of good times shared with the dead. It is distressing and confusing to children to have someone they love die, disappear, and never be mentioned again.

Children know when they've inquired about something that makes adults uncomfortable. They recognize that gasp and the body language grown-ups use...like the time they asked loudly what the letters in crayon on the wall in the McDonald's bathroom said. Adults quickly shush them up and then leave them wondering what relationship exists between crayon markings on the wall and their uncle, who was killed last month in a car crash. Talking of the dead is good therapy for adults as well as children.

Though it is not necessary to dwell on every aspect of death, a simple, factual answer is what children need and deserve. "Death happens when the body gets too worn out to work anymore. Sometimes it happens because of a bad accident. Everyone thinks about it sometimes and gets a little scared, but it usually doesn't happen to people until they are very old." This, with a reassuring hug, is all that most children need.

Many young children will not be faced with the death of someone they know and love. Still, the idea should not be foreign to them. Living with pets is an excellent way for children to become acquainted with cycles of life and death. Two excellent books to share with your child are _The Tenth Good Thing About Barney_ by Judith Viorst and _Nana Upstairs, Nana Downstairs_ by Tomi DiPaola. For adults wanting more information in this area, I suggest Ross's aforementioned book, as well as her own recommendations _Teaching Your Child to Cope With Crisis_ by Suzanne Ramos and _Helping Your Child to Understand Death_ by Anna Wolf.

To a Child, Divorce Stinks

Children's libraries today offer a wonderful selection of books on families that include single-parent households, blended families, families with many siblings, and families with none. There are stories which sensitively follow a family from stormy times through a divorce and finally into a stable, but changed, lifestyle. Without being cute or patronizing, these books conclude with an acceptable, if not happy, ending. We are left with the knowledge, from the child's perspective, that divorce is something we can learn to cope with, and that it can often be an improvement, but that it is always painful for everyone involved.

Why is this so important? Because many of us are uninformed about the effects of divorce on families. Often, when it becomes a personal issue, we rationalize its impact. "Children are adaptable," we say, to make our decisions less painful to live with.

As the divorce rate began its staggering ascent in this country about two decades ago, it was accompanied by a rationale that divorce was much easier on children than living in a violent home, or one where parents did not care about each other. Though this is often absolutely true, it is, at best, an incomplete analysis of the situation for families.

Many of us grew up in "family" neighborhoods where divorce was not a household word. Our parents firmly believed that marriage was forever, even if that meant a lifetime of abuse, alcoholism, or mental cruelty. With good reason, these notions were challenged and broken down. Divorce became a household word across America. The idea of "staying together for the sake of the children" was scorned by the general public. And couples, in record numbers, divorced—putting the United States in first place among Western industrialized nations for the highest divorce rate.

Recently that rate has shown a slight drop, indicating the first stabilizing trend in twenty years. We are beginning to reach a balance in both our statistics and our attitudes. We have moved away from the provincial notion that couples always marry for life. We have begun to accept that divorce is here to stay; that it often transforms a family in a positive way. But we also are moving away from the trend of treating the issue lightly; of glibly stating, "We'll all be much happier this way." We are now trying to look realistically at divorce as a traumatic event in the lives of families, like moving, death, long-term illness, new siblings, or other ordinary life stresses. We are studying its impact on children and seeking ways to make a difficult situation as tolerable as possible for all family members.

We've learned a great deal in the past two decades, mostly from listening to children talk about their feelings as their families went in new directions.

- We know that almost all children experience guilt and feel responsible for the divorce.
- We know that very young children frequently revert to earlier developmental stages during the process of divorce (toileting, thumb sucking, tantrums).
- We know that school-age children often are unable to concentrate on school work, or express anxiety through loss of appetite, diarrhea, or sleep problems.
- We know that teenagers tend to be affected as intensely as younger children, but communicate less to parents about their concerns. Research indicates that boys find it more difficult to adapt to these stresses than girls.
- We know that children of all ages fantasize that reconciliation can be achieved.

Given the facts on divorce now available to us, there are many things we can do to minimize the stress of divorce on children. It is best if both parents talk to children about the divorce. Studies indicate that women are often left with this task. If parents talk to children together, there is less opportunity for fault-finding, which always puts children in an unfair situation.

Human nature being what it is, it's naïve to hope that we can weather this storm without expressions of anger or hostility. However, a supportive emotional climate where children are encouraged to discuss their fears, disappointments, and concerns is helpful. Although an atmosphere of love and approval from both parents is crucial, presenting divorce in an upbeat, sprightly fashion is as unfair to children as was the old getting-your-tonsils-out-will-be-fun; you-can-have-all-the-ice-cream-you-want routine. Divorce is not fun and shouldn't be presented as such.

Expressions of hope that the divorce will bring an end to certain conflicts are appropriate as long as the realization of how hard this will be for a while is also discussed. The idea that "you're not losing a father, you're gaining a second home" may be easier on the divorcing couple, but is not much consolation to a child who still wishes her parents would stay together. We can all be more supportive of families in transition by avoiding the use of the expression "broken home." Even the youngest of children knows what "broken" means; something doesn't work anymore. We throw away broken toys or dishes. They are no good.

Today, blended families make up the largest growing percentage of families in America. Children in these families need the same positive self-image as anyone else. The same is true of single-parent families. As Antoinette Bosco has said in *Successful Single Parenting*, "A family in which there is a sense of unity, peace, comfort, mutual support and the unquestionable presence of love is whole, not broken—regardless of whether it is headed by one or two parents."

Moving Forward, Looking Back

School is out. It's vacation time, relaxation time, and, for one of every five families in America, it's moving time. Spring sees its portion of "For Sale" signs marked "Sold," and the moving vans take over in early summer, as nearly forty million families in the United States relocate.

Statistically, the most common reason for changing homes is parental job change. Other reasons often cited are the search for a more appropriate environment for raising children, a change in financial situation, a desire to live in a more urban or rural setting, and a departure from the present lifestyle. Whatever our reasons, the United States is the most mobile nation on earth.

Information on relocation tells us that men adapt more easily to moving than women. Frequently, the effects of moving on children are completely overlooked, or lost in the shuffle. We are quick to tell ourselves that children adapt easily to new situations. We are quick to tell our children that they will make new friends, enjoy their new school, or have a much bigger bedroom—without preparing them for the loneliness they might feel, or the inevitable sense of loss for their old friendships or old neighborhood.

Women often find it more difficult in a new community because, even in the nineties, it is primarily the moms who manage pediatricians, car pools, child care, and groceries. Adjusting to new circumstances is a challenge for anyone, but especially for homemakers. We forget how much we rely on the same old routine for efficiency. Most of us shop at the same supermarket at a certain time each week. We know which hours are too busy, when fresh produce comes in, and when there are long lines at the checkout. We learn which pediatricians call children by name, speak directly to them, and honestly assert, "This is going to hurt a bit." We know the quickest way to get from work to the child care center and elementary school without losing time in traffic jams. When we move, all of this changes. Errands take longer. Shopping is confusing. We have to begin a new routine. The transition is sometimes stressful.

Children, too, like their familiar routines. They know which times their favorite programs are on television and which channels to flip to. They know which yards they can take a shortcut through without getting yelled at. They know which store will give them the candy for thirty-seven cents because three pennies rolled away when they fell off their skateboards. They know the custodian at school or the cook at day care by name.

When they move, all of this changes. Making a transition is hard on kids. We can ease the strain of relocation on children by being supportive and enthusiastic about the new community, but realistic about the pain of parting with friends and familiar surroundings.

Although we often are not in a position of preference when timing a move for the family, if we do have a choice, there are a few guidelines we can follow. According to child psychologist Charles Schaefer, children under the age of eleven find moving less stressful than older children. If a child is close to graduation from grammar school or high school, letting her complete the year with her class is easier than forcing her to spend three or four months in a new school and graduate with strangers. Often, families can arrange for the youngster to live with relatives or friends for a few months, rather than change schools midyear.

Schaefer suggests that parents of very young children strive to make the new bedroom resemble the old one as closely as possible. If curtains, spreads, and furniture placement are the same, the child will be more comfortable in her new surroundings.

For parents of adolescents, a moving budget that allows for moderate long-distance calling to old friends will be much appreciated. Another way to relieve relocation depression for teenagers, if the budget allows, is with an invitation (with a round-trip bus ticket included) to a close friend from the old neighborhood.

No matter how exciting a move to a new area can be, almost all of us feel as though we are leaving a bit of ourselves behind when we move on. It is important for parents to allow children to experience the sadness, anger, or irritability that are common emotional responses to change.

Teaching Young Children About Sex

The parent of a first-grader recently expressed her dismay to me on the subject of sex education. "You know," she confided, "we have had to talk to our daughter about absolutely everything this year because of all the talk that goes on in the school yard! I think it's a shame when the world is such that if you don't tell your child about the facts of life, she'll come home from kindergarten with somebody else's version!"

Though I understand this mother's concern, I couldn't disagree with her perspective more. It points out one of the greater misunderstandings about young children and sexuality that our culture shares. It focuses on information as the heart of sex education, ignoring attitudes and parental modeling.

Though some of it is unconscious, we are teaching our children about sex from the moment they are born. We teach them through our touch, our words, our body language. We teach them about sexuality in the way we relate to them, to our spouses, and to our friends of the same and the opposite sex. Long before children begin school, they have learned that their family regards sex as an important and gratifying part of life, or as something quite unmentionable, or as something funny and a little nasty that is the butt of frequent jokes and asides.

Babies explore their world through touch. In infancy they discover the pleasurable sensations of their own bodies. Young children masturbate. How parents react to this affects not only the behavior of the moment but also the child's developing sexuality, which accompanies her to adulthood. Sometimes the failure to achieve sexual satisfaction in adult life can be traced to parental reactions to the child's discovery of her own body as a source of pleasure.

Most of us are aware of repressive or ignorant attitudes about sex that were fostered in our own childhoods. We don't want sex to be a problem for our children. Yet often we are full of uncertainty about our parental actions and reactions surrounding sex and our children. Should we allow our child to see us in the nude? Should the bathroom door be open or closed? What about bringing the baby into bed with us? Should we ignore, accept, or put a stop to our child's masturbation? How do we know the way to handle these situations?

It should be encouraging to know that there is no one right way to deal with sexual issues and your youngster. Child development experts agree that it is not usually what is done but how it is done that makes a lasting impression on young children.

On the issue of parental nudity, Dr. Mary Calderone makes this point in *The Family Book About Sexuality*: "What nudity does is make it easier for children to become absolutely certain about just how men and women are made. Children whose parents are at ease in such natural events as stepping out of the shower, toweling, and walking back to their room to dress are fortunate." However, Dr. Calderone is quick to admit that parents who feel uneasy about nudity have every right to their privacy and should not try to force behavior which makes them uncomfortable. It is not the nudity or lack of it that is so essential, but the positive, matter-of-fact way in which parents present themselves and their values.

Another concern of many parents is what to do if their young child walks in when they are making love. Obviously, the best idea is prevention. Adults who live with young children should be in the habit of locking the bedroom door when they make love. However, it is reassuring to know that great numbers of children see this event every year without being damaged for life. A response of anger or indignation is inappropriate in this situation. The child probably feels surprised or uncomfortable and would benefit from parental attempts to put her at ease. If possible, a simple comment like, "We are wanting to hold each other right now and would like you to go back to bed," can be a beginning lesson in privacy and intimacy for your child.

Another important consideration is that we can teach much by what we choose to say. For instance, parents go to great lengths to teach their babies the names of the eyes, ears, nose, teeth, tongue, hair, eyebrows, and chin, but often after this rather complete litany go to elbows, hands, knees, feet, and toes, totally excluding genitalia. This silence is making a loud statement: UNMENTIONABLE! Children should be taught the names of all their body parts.

As a supervisor of preschool teachers I often noticed student teachers leaving this same gap in their lessons on body parts. If I questioned them on it, the response was always the same: "I was afraid if I included penis, vagina, or breast that parents might come in and ask what I thought I was doing and I wouldn't know what to say." My advice was that it was their responsibility to teach all the parts of the body, and that if parents questioned their lesson, the response should be the same for "penis" as it is for "ear": it's important for children to know what their body has and what it does.

One of the sad facts about contemporary society is that sexuality is exploited everywhere. There is sex in newspaper and magazine advertising, sex on billboards, and sex on TV. Too often we make the assumption that because sex is everywhere, or because children use words that might indicate knowledge of sexuality, they have an understanding of sexual issues that we did not have in childhood. They do not.

Today's children, perhaps more than any previous generation, are in need of lots of attention, caring, and talking on the part of their parents concerning issues of sexuality. They need to see and hear from their parents that sex is important; that it goes hand-in-hand with respect and caring. They need factual information and parental protection from the media bombardment that frequently degrades human sexuality. Today's children need parents who will teach what they believe in a relaxed and thoughtful manner. They need parents who can accept that sexuality—with its talking, cuddling, masturbating, and play—is all a natural, healthy experience of growing.

5

School Days

Two Different Worlds: Home and School

It's six o'clock. The bank across from McDonald's says it's ninety-two degrees. Cars pour into the parking lot. Inside, the supper hour is in full gear. Babies are crying. Two-year-olds pound high chair trays. A four-year-old sent for straws returns with forty. A young family settles at a table near the rest rooms; their five-year-old is known to make as many as three trips to the facilities in a half-hour. The mom looks around, thinking, "Starvation might be more relaxing than this."

The dad looks around and comments, "Any couple contemplating parenthood who stops in here for a burger will put off a family forever!"

"How soon you forget," she chides him. "Any couple contemplating parenthood will look around and think, 'When we have children, they'll never act like this!'" He recognizes the truth in her comment and they laugh together.

These moments are common to parenting: the noise, the fatigue, the disorder, and the humor of it all. When friends wrestling with the decision of whether to have children ask if we would do it all again, we often pause too long before responding. We know, now, how difficult the job is. We have mixed feelings sometimes about the intensity of the emotions involved. We find it easy to talk about the hard economic realities of raising children. We can be frank about the frustrations of interrupted careers or inadequate child care facilities. Yet putting the specific joys of our parenting into words is a difficult task.

Often we are amazed when a habit that drove us crazy in a niece or neighbor child is tolerable in our own child. What Grandpa views as insolence, we interpret as wit. What a stranger sees as overactive, we see as energy. Mostly, parents love their children and see them as very special individuals. We might wish that Susan would work harder in school, or Jeff would help out more at home...but even if they don't, we love them, anyway.

"Home," Robert Frost wrote, "is the place where, when you have to go there, they have to take you in....Something you somehow haven't to deserve."

When homes are functioning well, the people within them feel accepted just because they are there. It's not a matter of "deserving" that comfort because one is honest or hardworking or good, but merely because one _is_.

Each September our children leave the comforts of home for that other world of school. They move from the private world of unconditional love to the public world where their acceptance depends largely on their performance. They are measured by standardized tests and judged against the performance of classmates.

There was a time when most homes and schools agreed upon what was good for children. This is no longer the case. What is valued varies from home to home and from classroom to classroom within the same school system. This fact creates stress for many parents, teachers, and children. There has long been a theory that parents and teachers should back each other up, providing a unified front for the children. I don't think this is always possible in a pluralistic society. However, I don't think differences of opinion between parents and teachers need to have difficult side effects for children. If the adults can agree to disagree, children can learn a lesson in human relations along with their social studies.

It is difficult for parents who encourage inquiry in their children to have this questioning considered rebelliousness at school. It is difficult for parents who have reared children to respect authority—no matter what—to have teachers encouraging students to challenge, probe, or question the validity of governments or traditional values.

We no longer live in an era where roles and responsibilities are clear-cut. What we sometimes forget is how adaptable children are. Children quickly learn that Grandpa can be talked into an extra half-hour at night while Dad says, "Brush your teeth and go to bed." They know that at Jason's house you can make a fort out of the furniture, and at Jonathan's you leave your shoes in the hall so you won't dirty the carpet. They can also adjust to parent/teacher styles which are not complementary.

Parents should feel comfortable saying to their child, "I quite disagree with that approach, but it is your teacher's job to decide what goes on at school...and it's your job to live by the school rules while at school."

Teachers should feel comfortable saying, "Your parent knows what she is comfortable with at home, but here I expect you to raise your hand before speaking," "...refrain from profanity in the classroom," "...have your work completed on time," etc.

Research indicates that the family has the major impact on the educational outcome of its children. Parental interest is necessary to maintain the child's learning success. So collaboration of parents and teachers is crucial to effectively educating our youngsters. Collaboration doesn't mean agreeing on everything, but merely trying to respect each other's perspectives. Teachers sometimes feel they are expected to have all the answers. Parents sometimes feel their child's every action is a personal reflection on their parenting abilities. Neither is true. Parents and teachers can best help the children they mutually care about by establishing open, honest lines of communication early in September.

It is a special day for teachers when a parent stops in just to say hello or to offer his or her interest and support. Most teachers are aware that parents are their best resource in reinforcing what the school wants the child to learn. The wise teacher involves parents in their child's schooling in a meaningful way. The wise parent gets acquainted at the beginning of the year with his child's teacher. A plant, a book on child development, or time, if you have it to volunteer, lets your child's teacher know that you appreciate his or her efforts.

When parents and teachers have come together in these positive ways in the beginning of the year, it will be easier to problem-solve as a team later on. Parents and teachers, as partners, are a powerful force for shaping the future of individual children and the schools they attend.

Get Ready, Get Set...Go!

It's Tony's first day of school. He has a new plaid shirt, polished shoes, a fresh haircut, and a scared-to-death expression on his face. "I can't understand Tony's behavior today," his mother confides to the first-grade teacher. "No one could be better prepared for school than Tony. Why, he's known his ABC's since he was two years old. He reads well and has done basic math at home for more than a year."

In a nearby group of anxious parents and first-graders, Sara's mother overhears the comments made by Tony's mom. "Oh, no!" she thinks to herself. "Poor Sara doesn't know a Q from a Z and can't even write her name."

Sara, unaware of her mother's concern, has struck up a conversation with some of the children. "Did you know that a guy in California once ate seventeen bananas in two minutes?" she offers to anyone who chooses to listen. Several children giggle. A few let go of parents' hands. Others continue to cling, knuckles white, eyes brimming with tears. It's a familiar scene on that all-important first day of school.

For those of us who have survived the experience of sending our firstborn off to school, there are memories, good and bad. Wasn't it a sinking feeling when you were counting on—at least—a backward glance, but your six-year-old matter-of-factly stated, "You stay in the car. I'm big enough to go on from here by myself!"?

Or maybe you recall the special breakfast on that eventful morning that was interrupted by your child announcing in panic, "I think I'm going to throw up!"

Charles M. Schultz captures some of those back-to-school anxieties in the "Peanuts" comic strip, when Charlie Brown exclaims, "My brain doesn't mind school at all...it's my stomach that hates it!"

What is it that makes some children skip off to school in happy anticipation while others hold back, crying, sucking thumbs, and begging for Dad or Mom? What can parents do to help their children get off to a good start? Are there certain pitfalls we can avoid?

First, we must acknowledge that each child is an individual in her own right. Since we are comfortable accepting that children walk, talk, acquire teeth, and pedal a tricycle at different ages, why should we expect all youngsters to be ready and eager for schooling at exactly the same age?

We must also examine the myths, widely and erroneously accepted as fact by many parents, surrounding the education of young children. Most prevalent among these myths are:

- How much children know before entering school indicates the measure of success they will experience in class.
- Intelligence is the main ingredient of school success.
- An early start in academics leads to later school success.

Since most parents truly want what is best for their children, it is alarming to note that many parents believe that children can and indeed should be forced to learn. They spend the preschool years teaching their children facts and academic skills, while overlooking far more important areas of learning. In *The Child Under Six*, educator James L. Hymes, Jr. writes, "We worry needlessly about reading and, because we worry, we jump the gun! So often we mess up the teaching of reading the way we earlier complicated toilet training, training in property rights, and eating habits. Just as we produce too many children who resist food and resist sleep, we turn out too many who resist reading."

Let's look again at our first-graders in the school yard. Tony knows his letters and reads books, yet clings to his parent and won't join the other children. Sara, who doesn't know a Q from a Z, is mastering a far more crucial skill: reading human behavior. No doubt she endeared herself to her peers by tossing out a funny fact at a time when tensions were running high. If a child has learned something about moods and human frailty in her preschool years, she is more likely to be accepting of herself and the people around her.

Another important skill required for success in school is the ability to accept failure as an inevitable part of growing and learning. The child who can casually say, "I did an awful job on this; I think I'll try again," is truly ready for the task of polishing academic skills.

Perhaps the most necessary skill is the ability to understand the difference between thoughts and actions. If a child expresses anger, fear, or frustration in regard to the school situation, he needs to have those feelings accepted before he can work through them. Yet so often we unwittingly say, "Don't be afraid!" or "Now, you don't mean that," when, of course, the child does mean it and we should respect his feelings. When a child knows that he is accepted just as he is, he will feel good about himself and most likely get along well with others. It is important for the child to know that being mad at a classmate is okay, but kicking him in the stomach is not an acceptable way to express that anger!

It is natural for parents to experience a bit of anxiety over their child's success in school. But frequently we worry needlessly about academic achievement, forgetting that it is only a part of school success. There are several things we can do to eliminate stress on that first big day and throughout the early weeks of school.

65

The back-to-school wardrobe may have real significance. For some children, a brand-new outfit which they are able to select is a real delight. Other children, however, would do better to wear a comfortable old T-shirt, jeans, and sneakers: if a youngster is feeling strange about a new situation, old, favorite clothes can be a real comfort. It's also important for all young children to have clothes which enable the freedom of movement so natural to the primary-grade child. If a child wears comfortable jerseys, pants, and sneakers, she is free to run, jump, hang by her knees, and fall without scraping knees and ruining clothes. If a child wears fancy dresses and leather-soled shoes, she learns to passively watch the action of others.

As parents, we like the feeling of sending our children off to school with a stomach full of hot oatmeal, eggs, or fruit. Breakfast is certainly important, but on that first day, if there are protests, it's a good idea to respect them. After all, how often have you said, "I couldn't eat a thing!" before a job interview, important meeting, or presentation?

If you're having trouble with ideas for school lunches, Vicki Lansky's cookbooks, *Feed Me, I'm Young* and *The Taming of the Candy Monster* offer nutritious recipes for meals and snacks.

For the child without previous school experience, a visit to the school a week before class begins can be reassuring. Reading stories about school can also give the young child an idea of what to expect. *First Day in School* by Bill Birzin, *Will I Have a Friend?* and *When Will I Read?* by Miriam Cohen, and *Willy Bear* by Mildred Kantrowitz are excellent books to share with your child before her big day.

Although the initial school experience seems to demand more of younger children and their parents, we mustn't forget the difficulty which older children experience each year as they adjust to schedules, homework, earlier bedtimes, and the general academic pressures school presents. They need our support, extra patience, and a bit of humor to help them get back into their school routine.

Parents will find flexibility and a sense of humor most valuable in adjusting to the changes which greater independence and being out in the world bring to their school-age children. When my oldest son entered school, a memo was sent home to inform parents of general school policy, snow holidays, bus schedules, and the like. At the bottom of the last page, the principal had printed, with good humor, "We promise to take seriously only half of the 'home stories' if you'll grant us the same courtesy on the 'school stories.'" I wasn't quite sure what she meant.

Two days later, Sean said he'd done a "talking" report on "My Summer Vacation."

I questioned him eagerly, "Did you talk about the big jet?"

"No," he replied.

"Did you tell them about the cable cars in San Francisco?"

"Nope, I forgot!"

"You must have mentioned the redwood trees?"

"I forgot that, too."

"Well, Sean," I said, finally exasperated, "What did you tell them?"

"I told them," he beamed triumphantly, "how lucky we were to have round-trip tickets, since you lost all your money in Reno!" In that instant, I knew what the principal meant. We laughed a little, but we sent his lunch money in immediately!

Beginnings:
Getting Ready for First Grade

Have you ever noticed a particular tone of voice used by parents to describe the joys of public education to a soon-to-be first-grader? It closely resembles the voice we once used to tell her how big and strong she would grow if she would just eat spinach. I think in advertising they call it "oversell."

Though I'm convinced that we can develop a taste for spinach and schooling, I also believe that both can sometimes be hard to swallow at age six.

Often, in the flurry of preparation for this big event, we overlook some important facts that need to be discussed. For instance, while parents talk with enthusiasm about the "fun" their youngsters will have in first grade, they often fail to mention that it is a permanent commitment—even if one is not as delighted with the arrangements as one had hoped to be.

This point was made clear to me when my oldest son came home in October of his first year and announced calmly, "It's not much like I thought it would be, so I've decided to go back to kindergarten." Sean had equated first grade with story hour at the library or play group or any of the other optional activities he had taken part in. We had done nothing to help him understand otherwise. At that point, we all had a difficult time adjusting; a situation which might have been avoided if we had talked more explicitly about what going to school really meant.

Children usually accept that parents have to go to work, even though they often wish we could stay home to play. They usually accept that they must go to bed, even though they wish they could stay up all night. They will also accept the school routine without much difficulty, but it's a good idea to let them know from the start that this is a permanent part of their day-to-day living.

The purchase of a backpack seems to be very significant to most six-year-olds. They will talk nonstop of the kinds of juice and sandwiches they plan to take to school. But once the big day comes and goes, parents begin to notice half-eaten sandwiches, untouched fruit, and even granola bars coming home in the new backpack. Don't despair!

Many children take a long time to get used to the school lunchroom. Unlike home, where mealtimes are often a family affair where ideas, jokes, and the day's doings are discussed, most schools discourage laughing and playing over lunch. This is not necessarily a philosophical point on the school's part, but one of practicality. In order for everyone to have cafeteria time, most children are rushed through lunch in a way that does not encourage one to enjoy a meal. Our answer to this has been a good breakfast and a hearty after-school snack, with a few encouraging words about how difficult it must be to be hurried through lunch when you really need a relaxing break.

Toileting can also be stressful for new first-graders. These regular routines, which are handled with sensitivity at home or day care, can be more difficult when children are on their own. Reassure your child that everyone is a little uneasy when facing new situations.

Carefully planning our response to our youngster's anxieties can make it easier on all of us. For example, saying, "It is a big building. I can see why you are afraid you will get lost. But I'm sure you'll manage...and if you do get frightened, one of the grown-ups at school will help you," is reassuring. To say, "Don't be silly. You won't get lost!" denies the child's feelings and increases her fears.

Similarly, we often pose questions after school which welcome a one-word answer...and then wonder why our kids don't talk to us. Instead of saying, "Did you have a good day?" ("Yes") or, "How was your day?" ("Fine"), you might try sitting down, establishing eye contact, and saying brightly, "Tell me about your day," or, "What was the most interesting thing you heard today?"

Parents should understand that when children feel uncertain about a new situation, it is a normal reaction for them to revert to younger behavior. Thus, many youngsters who have long given up thumbs, blankies, and clinging bring back the old habits those first few weeks of school. It's a good idea to accept the child's need for these comforts. Saying, "You're a big first-grader now—you don't need to suck your thumb," is the approach least likely to help your child through this transition. It is, indeed, being a "big first-grader" that has caused her to put her thumb back in her mouth! It will pass, probably before the leaves turn orange in October.

Starting school really does represent a big change for your child. It is a change most children welcome, yet one which always comes with mixed feelings for both parent and child. With care, we can help our youngsters deal with their fears and encourage them to enjoy this new challenge.

Making the Grade: What Is It Worth?

Report cards came out this month. Parents and children look to this day with pleasure or foreboding as they accept an assessment of learning and skills. Parents receive them with the hope that the evaluations were thoughtfully prepared to assess their child's progress.

It may be difficult for some parents to understand the particulars of these reports. It isn't hard, however, to get some general ideas about their impact on family life! I'm always fascinated as my children discuss who got what among their acquaintances...and what it means.

"Phil is on restriction again—this time for the whole grading period!"

"Jennifer Brown got fifty dollars from her father for making the honor roll."

"That's nothing—Mike Bresnehan's parents said he'd get a new dirt bike if he got all A's and B's, and he changed a D to a B and nobody even found out!"

"Kevin is depressed because his mother says he'll never get into Phillips Exeter Academy with grades like that."

My kids have always accepted that, though we care about what they do, we are pretty indifferent to report cards. There are a lot of reasons for this.

Because I've been a student most of my life, I've had lots of experience being graded. I'm able to look back and realize that, of all the grades I've received, about half were an accurate assessment of my effort and acquisition of knowledge. There were the B's received in college English without cracking a book because I'd read the requirements in high school. There was the course in graduate school that I easily aced: I never finished the text, but the term project was a written paper, something I do well. I remember that the course from which I learned the most was the course for which I received my lowest grade. This is not unusual. So many factors influence the dynamics of students, teachers, grades, and parental reactions.

I believe most educators are aware of the shortcomings of our methods of evaluation. The system that would make sense—a written evaluation of each student, based on her individual progress in relation to her ability and learning style—would take too long to prepare, and probably wouldn't be well received by parents, anyhow. Many school systems have returned to letter evaluations, on the request of parents who claim that letter grades are what they know and understand best.

Before feeling complacent about your child's academic success, however, or concerned about her lack of it, there are several things you might want to consider.

Learning is approached differently by different children, and also by the same child at different times. The match of child and teacher often affects how well a child will manage academically in a particular year. It is ludicrous to believe that teachers can be totally objective in evaluating students. It is equally ridiculous to tell ourselves that everyone begins on the same starting line in the race for the coveted A's. We rationalize that in America the opportunities are there for those who really want to seize them. Is this true?

- There is the child whose mother, a lawyer, conscientiously tries to help by making sure her child's work is "perfect" before it's handed in...a definite A!
- There is the child whose mother sleeps days and works nights, while her father works days and sleeps nights. On their combined income, they can scarcely afford rent and food. This child might study her geography more than others, but has no colored paper, glue, or markers at home, and can't get help from her overtired parents...a deprived A?
- There is the child whose father is an airline pilot who brings postcards and flags home from Paris for his son's report on France...a deserved A?

There is the whole question of ability, motivation, and achievement. Often a child capable of A work makes no effort and still receives a B due to her natural ability, or access to the right tools, or parental support; while another child's best effort brings only a C, yet she has actually produced the most she is capable of.

It is also true that neatness is a factor that carries a lot of weight in our grading system. We do not leave much room for the creative or gifted child who "marches to the beat of a different drummer." So often, handwriting or spelling brings down a child's grade on an interesting theme; yet in the adult world, everything is typed and edited, anyway. Is handwriting really an indication of what a child is learning?

How can we consider a report card an accurate assessment of progress when we measure every child by the same ruler, knowing that individual learning styles, natural ability, parental involvement, and socioeconomic status greatly influence a child's chances of succeeding? But how, you might ask, can parents find out what their children are learning if they do not take their child's report card as the ultimate indicator?

Talk with your children. Listen to them. Can they communicate well? Do they solve problems? When a plan doesn't work, do they seek alternative solutions? Do they have hobbies and interests? Do they read for enjoyment? Are they curious about what makes things happen? Can they accept failure as a part of learning and enthusiastically try again? Are they happy?

Dr. David Elkind of Tufts University has raised issues in his book *The Hurried Child* which should interest every parent. He cites our preoccupation with grades and achievement as one of the major causes of increased stress-related illness in childhood. Children are under pressure, and it's affecting their physical and emotional well-being. Elkind claims, "Pressuring children to get certain marks on tests that at best measure rote knowledge is hardly the way to improve the education of our children....Our educational establishment suffers from the same ills as did our industrial establishment: it has become too product-oriented and has ignored the workers."

Kenneth Keniston, author of *All Our Children: The American Family Under Pressure*, echoes Elkind's concerns: "We measure the success of schools not by the kinds of human beings they promote, but by whatever increases in reading scores they chalk up. We have allowed quantitative standards to become the principle yardstick for our definition of our children's worth." By accepting this, we fail ourselves and our children!

Talking to the Teacher:
It Still Isn't Easy

Each September, as children head back to school, parents are flooded with memories, anxieties, and more-than-usual bills from revolving charge accounts. As youngsters get used to alarm clocks, homework, and the end of summer's leisure, parents are hoping that this will be a happy, productive year for their children.

In recent years, schools and families both have endured a significant amount of social change and turmoil. Teachers feel that troubles with families are making their jobs more difficult. Parents are increasingly dissatisfied with the quality of their children's schooling. Thus, when parents and teachers meet, defenses are often up on both sides.

Sara Lightfoot Lawrence of Harvard University claims that parents' negative visions of schools often arise from their childhood memories of oppression and fear of the all-powerful teacher. This cannot be a factual portrait because it is based on faded impressions; but each generation passes these biases on to the next. Children enter school carrying not only their own apprehensions, but the weight of their parents' resentment of long-past school days. Lawrence suggests that it would take several decades of sensible, friendly teaching to remove this negative pattern among parents, children, and teachers. Unfortunately, because of these feelings and fears on both sides, parents and teachers often square off in silent resistance to open communication that could benefit families, schools, and communities.

Communication between parents and teachers can greatly enhance the quality of our children's school experiences. Both parents and teachers have been chastised by the media for not doing an adequate job for the children. As parents, you can encourage teachers merely by letting them know that you know it isn't an easy job, and that you appreciate the teacher's efforts on your child's behalf. Likewise, teachers can reassure parents.

Teachers are often expected to give the impression that all is well with the system. For years, it was assumed that teachers had all the answers. "I just don't know what to do!" was a socially unacceptable response to parents. That put an unfair burden on our teachers; sometimes answers are not easy to find. Sometimes the truth is painful. Parents need to give teachers the chance to make mistakes, too: certainly none of us would claim that we always know just what to do with our children.

Parents and teachers alike want what is good for the children. The point that is often overlooked is that what children need from parents and what they need from teachers is not always the same approach. Simply put, parents and teachers could help each other a lot by trying to imagine what the other's job is like.

Too often, parents feel that teachers do not understand their child's individual needs. They feel their child is treated as a number; the youngster at the back of the third row. But school is not like home. Parents cannot expect nor encourage their children to hope for the same level of attention or affection at school that they receive from their family. Part of adjusting to school is accepting one's role as part of a large classroom group and separating, to a certain extent, from the family for a portion of the day.

Similarly, teachers might stop hoping for parents to bring the same objectivity to conferences that teachers strive to achieve. The expression "love is blind" can apply to the parent/child relationship as easily as to that of lovers. Parents tend to think of their children as wonderful, and that's a blessing. Children need someone in their corner who always gives them the benefit of the doubt!

If parents could see that teachers are sometimes forced to view their child in reference to the group, and if teachers could accept that parents are pretty unlikely to see their children except in a very subjective way, it would help both parents and teachers to do a better job.

School Days—Happy Days?

At a recent meeting for parents of next year's ninth-graders, a guidance counselor suggested that we remember that fun should be one of the goals achieved throughout the high school years. There was a hesitance in her voice as she cautioned parents about working their offspring too hard. I recognized the hope for balance which we in the area of human services strive for when we act as liaison between parents who want success for their children and students who sometimes pay a serious price for meeting parental expectations.

There was a time when play and fun were so much a part of school days that teachers and parents occasionally had to prod youngsters to focus on their academics. Experts agree that this is no longer the case. All reports on the present quality of American public schools aside, students are under pressure to achieve, and they know it.

An elementary principal of many years recently told me that she rarely hears the giggling and playful laughter that used to mark the recess time. A retired elementary teacher remembered the singing which used to brighten every elementary school classroom. "Once, when I visited my grandson's classroom," she told me, "I asked the teacher why I never heard singing as I walked down the hallway. The teacher responded that the students had a special music period with the music teacher. She admitted quite sadly that even in the primary grades, there was no time for singing except when they went out for music."

This reminded me of my own teacher-training many years ago, when we were required to take Music for Elementary Teachers so that we would have a repertoire of songs to break up the day and the schedule of skill building. We were told that children needed this to maintain their energy and concentration levels.

Has this changed? I doubt it. Yet curriculum committees continue to make demands for stronger academic programs. Parents demand more homework, even in the early grades. It's as if we believe that taking away the pleasures of childhood will somehow increase our children's chance for success in adulthood.

At this recent meeting, parents quizzed school officials on their youngsters' schedules.

"How can my son get into college if he takes general math as a freshman?" one concerned father asked.

"Can't my daughter take an overload first semester? She's an excellent student, and we're shooting for early college admission," another commented.

"If a student is really capable," one mother insisted, "why can't she forge ahead?"

The adolescents who accompanied their parents to this meeting didn't look as interested in their futures right at this time as their parents would lead us to believe. There were the typical pimples, braces, and shy smiles. One father claimed, "My daughter is determined to be a veterinarian."

The teacher enthusiastically said to the young woman, "You must love science, then."

The student looked momentarily puzzled, then responded, "Oh, no...but I just love horses!"

The evening news too often reports teenage suicides. One such case in Chicago involved upper-middle class youngsters whose parents conscientiously tried to provide the best of everything, including the promise of tuition for Ivy League schools, if the youngsters would just keep up their grades. In a poignant interview with the father of one of the victims, the feeling of confusion and deep pain came through. He shook his head sadly and said, "It makes no sense. He had everything to live for. What makes a successful young man take his own life?"

Some professionals link the increase in adolescent suicide to the pursuit of success. There was a straight-A student who hung herself after receiving a B. In her suicide note she stated, "Mom and Dad have never said anything to me about having to get good grades. In fact, we rarely talk about it. But I know they do not want, nor could they tolerate, a failure. And if I fail in what I do, I fail in what I am." It is clear that the pressure is not always spoken, but youngsters sense it, anyway.

Many parents quickly put a stop to compulsive eating of junk food, too much TV, or too many extracurricular activities. Yet how often do we let our adolescents "burn the midnight oil," missing much-needed rest to pursue that coveted spot in the National Honor Society?

It is natural and appropriate for parents to want their children to succeed in life. Education is one of the tools for reaching that goal. But if our children are to succeed, one of the gifts we must give them is the ability to separate who they are from what they accomplish.

6

It's Child's Play

William's Doll and Wendy's Workbench

A recent conversation with a friend started me thinking about stereotypical playthings for children. It seems her friend had talked about the negative effects of too many trucks on little boys. I listened thoughtfully as my friend discussed the macho image and Tonka trucks. "Could I be guilty of fostering the macho image in my own home?" I wondered as I walked across our backyards.

Sitting in my family room (decorated in early truck), I watched my four-year-old line up every cylindrical container he could find. He was vigorously involved in playing "garbage man," loading his truck and driving it across the room to leave his load at "the dump." When we take a bike ride, we stop at every building site to watch workers and trucks. When we read books, they are truck books. Though his drawings are primitive still, his ideas are not. "Here is the engine," he says as he scribbles. "And now the wheels—it's front-wheel drive."

Do you try to interest him in other things, you may be wondering?

Not too much. Right now his world is full of the sounds of trucks, their functions, their drivers, their wheels. I delight in watching him pursue it endlessly.

On the shelves in his bedroom are dolls of many varieties. There is the soft baby doll we put in his crib before he was born. There are Raggedy Andy, Bert, and Ernie. There's a doll (custom made) with eyes and hair like his, bought on Cape Cod for his first Christmas. On his first birthday we bought the Italian-made "anatomically correct" baby doll so he could relate to a doll of his own sex. He has a crib, a high chair, and other "fathering" props. But the fact is, he's just not interested. So we don't buy dolls anymore.

My older son was another story. Offered the same variety of playthings, he loved his dolls. I endured the looks (and comments) of relatives who felt his interest inappropriate. When I selected a carriage for his "family" for his third birthday, the salesperson beamed. "She'll love it!" he said. I paid and left.

I delighted in watching this child "father" his brood. We continued to surprise him on special occasions with a new doll, until finally his interests turned to the activities of basketball, carpentry, and chemistry.

As a child, I loved dolls. Every year at holiday time, I waited in eager anticipation for my newest arrival. My good friend, now a chemical analyst, yearned for erector sets, chemicals, an electric train. She got dolls instead. She hated them. Every year she would ask for the train or the chemistry set, and would not even feign excitement at the dolls she continued to receive. Despite her lack of interest in nurturing play as a youngster, today she is a loving and competent mother.

The point is, our goal as parents should be to carefully consider the individual interests of a child when purchasing playthings. All children should be exposed to woodworking, trucks, dolls, puppets, dishes and pots, climbing and riding toys, and good books.

However, children have their own unique temperaments, interests, and levels of physical activity. Some children prefer books, painting, and table games to climbing, riding and ball games. Some of these children are girls; some are boys. Some children prefer nurturing play with dolls and stuffed toys to motor sounds, trucks, and cars. Some of these children are boys, and some are girls.

All too often in the past, boys and girls were directed to "appropriate sex-role" activities. Tomboys and sissies were tolerated, while parents hoped that the stage would pass quickly. Today, many parents are trying to raise their children free from sex-role stereotypes. We conscientiously offer many different experiences to our children.

Yet recently, I've noticed parents trying too hard. A mother confided to me, "You know, I'm so embarrassed. I've bought her a stethoscope, building blocks, dump trucks, and trains, and all she wants to play with are dolls!"

Another mother I know bought her five-year-old son the book *William's Doll* and a baby doll, when what he wanted "most in the world," he said, was "a set of real tools and a whole bunch of wood!"

Every child should have the opportunity to sample a variety of activities and playthings. But each child should also have the right to say, "I don't want to play with that. I want to play with this," and have the adults in her life respect her wishes. A few points to remember when purchasing playthings:

- Toys that children can be actively involved with are preferable to toys that are passively watched. Examples of action toys: Legos, Playmobil Systems, clay, paints, models, and building blocks.
- Often, battery-operated toys have a single use. Children tire of them quickly.
- Dolls and stuffed toys that are cuddly and depend on your son's or daughter's imagination to "come to life" are better than the walking, talking variety.
- Large trucks of durable composition are loved by preschoolers. Avoid the battery-operated variety which offer motor sounds. Listen to girls and boys from ages two to six—they are great with motor sounds and prefer to make their own.

Gifts for Kids, Powered by Love

Erma Bombeck refers to the great holiday purchasing program as "the game you can't win."

"If it isn't under your tree on Christmas Day," she writes, "you are an unfit parent and your child will grow up to rob convenience stores wearing pantyhose over his face."

Parents struggle with issues of materialism all year in regard to their child's wants and needs. But the pressure becomes greatest during the holiday season. There are many reasons for this. First, of course, is the media hype. Before the leaves start to change, the networks begin their massive advertising campaigns. Children are convinced by media magic that their lives will be more adventurous, fun, or important if they just have this toy or that game. Now it's their turn to apply pressure to the parents: "I'm the only one at school who doesn't have it," "It's the only thing I want this year."

Parents are vulnerable to the pressure. So often we succumb to it even when we know the desired objects are not worth the price, will be disappointing compared to the commercial representation, and will end up at a garage sale with all the other items in which our children have lost interest. So why do we do it? The response is, of course, "So we don't disappoint the children." It's time that we parents took a closer look at some of our motives.

The old joke about Dad buying the electric train for his son but playing with it himself still rings true. Though the Lionels have given way to computer games and VCRs, the rationale is similar. We often try to fill old voids from our own childhoods at holiday time. Or we want our children to be among the lucky ones who are trendsetters with the latest game craze. Or we overspend with credit cards to ease a painful conscience because we underspend time with our children.

Children look to parents for a sense of what is reasonable; for a sense of order. Contrary to the conventional wisdom about disappointing the children, most youngsters are delighted with a gift that is resourceful or unique.

Hobby shops are full of engaging gifts for children. There are woodburning and leathercraft sets, stained glass kits, and printing kits, all at prices that make more sense than those of the heavily advertised items. Any youngster five to ten years of age would be delighted with a canvas bag filled with scrap wood and a set of real tools. Add some sandpaper, nails, and a carpenter's hat—a perfect gift!

For the young chef at your house, you might try filling a basket with a juvenile cookbook, the ingredients necessary for several recipes, some wooden spoons, wire whips, and a personalized apron.

Today it is economical enough to outfit even the youngest photographer with a first camera, several rolls of film, and a photo album for the finished product.

An embroidery basket is another excellent and inexpensive way to please a child on your list. There are many sets for beginners, with patterns, hoops, floss, needles, and directions.

All of the above suggestions operate without batteries, but require an essential ingredient—adult supervision. These are gifts for adults to share with children. Though the ideas are all "tested" child pleasers, that last ingredient is what makes them special holiday gifts: the memory of the time spent together.

Coaching the Kids Through Summer

"School's Out—Drive Carefully," the bumper sticker cautions us. "Don't Forget the Sun Block," the American Cancer Society warns; that well-loved fun in the sun can be hazardous to your health. Public service announcements remind us of the dangers of drinking and driving, or drinking and swimming, on those long holiday weekends.

But what about the children? Accidents are the leading cause of death among children five to thirteen years of age. The accident rate is highest during the summer vacation months. Some of these fatalities could be avoided.

We are often uncomfortable discussing danger with our children; we don't want to scare them. Yet we want to ensure their safety. Not only are we concerned about swimming, driving, and biking safety, but also about peer pressure, sexual abuse of children, and drug and alcohol use among the very young.

How much can we say without sounding cynical and pessimistic? In today's world, children need more than the old never-take-candy-from-a-stranger routine. Today's verbally sophisticated youngsters make it easy for parents to assume there is a level of understanding that is not really there. For instance, many five- or six-year-olds will tell you that you should never speak to strangers. However, when asked to explain the word "stranger," the same youngsters will describe giants, monsters, or creepy creatures that lurk in the dark. They would not classify a woman, man, or teenager that they don't know as a stranger. Parents need to make it clear that a stranger is anyone a child has not met at home or at school.

Parents are often surprised at their youngster's difficulty in understanding that he or she is not the only Jason or Heather in the world. A child's name is so significant to her that she's liable to go anywhere with an adult who calls her by it. For this reason, personalized clothing, backpacks, and the like should be avoided. These items give a potential child abuser an extra "in." More importantly, a child should be told that just because a stranger knows her name, it doesn't mean he knows her.

Sexual abuse of children is a fear many parents have, yet often it is a topic not directly discussed with the young. Research indicates that in the majority of sexual abuse cases, the offender is a relative, friend, or neighborhood acquaintance, well known to the child. For this reason, it is crucial that parents explain openly to children the nature of sexual abuse.

A child should know that certain behavior is inappropriate from friend or stranger. The idea of "body space" is understandable even to a very young child. Explaining that we don't allow anyone to touch our penis or vagina because it is our own private space is simple enough. If using direct anatomical terms is uncomfortable for parents, body space can be defined as "the part of your body covered by your swimsuit (or underwear)." Young children should know to tell us at once if a friend or stranger invades their body space.

With older children, our concerns are not so much, "Will my child know what to do?" as, "Will my child have the courage to do what she knows she should?" The ten- to fourteen-year age group ranks highest in the summer accident rate for children. This is the age of dares. It is often the age of initial experimentation with drugs, alcohol, and sex. With the majority of parents of school-age children employed full time, summer often provides long hours of unsupervised time in empty houses. Parents and children need to talk about rules, expectations, and supervision.

It is difficult for kids at this age to say no, even if they are also afraid of saying yes. Most adolescents can't bring themselves to say, "I can't do that—my mother wouldn't want me to." *Parents* magazine suggests practicing some hypothetical situations with your kids, in which they can prepare some good responses. For instance, if the group suggests diving off rocks at the beach and your child has been taught that it's a safety hazard, she might respond, "I'll visit you at the hospital!" instead of, "It's dangerous; I'm not allowed to do it."

Bicycle safety should be reviewed with children as summer approaches. Identification is important for children who are "about town" on their own. My kids all wear "dog tags" purchased reasonably at Personal Touch; name, address, and phone number are engraved on a disc and worn on a chain around the neck. A physician friend recently pointed out that blood type would be a good idea, too. Such information could save a child's life in a medical emergency.

Take some time soon with your children to talk about the hazards that could interfere with a safe and happy summer. Prepare them for possible dangers and tell them exactly what your expectations are. Then *enjoy*. But drive carefully...and don't forget the sun block.

Trust and Caution: Striking a Balance

When I was a child, milk came in bottles. There was always a certain fear of breaking one, but the milkman was a great friend to the neighborhood kids. When it was really hot, he sometimes gave us chunks of ice to suck on. Today, during breakfast, children look at milk cartons that carry pictures of missing children. Some offer preventive measures for avoiding the national epidemic of missing children.

The word "prevent" is a strong one. We cannot prevent the tragedy of missing children, any more than we can prevent floods or blizzards. In other words, we can and must take every precautionary measure possible, but sometimes those things happen. We feel angry; we feel powerless. But they happen.

Certainly, the recent attempt by schools to insist that parents call in if their children are to be late or absent is a sound one. The idea that families establish a code word to be used if anyone other than family picks a child up from school or recreational activities has some merit. However, I sometimes compare it to the old adage about good locks and security systems keeping honest people out. I can picture a situation where my spouse cannot be reached and my youngest child, burning with fever, refuses to leave the school with a good friend who has forgotten the password. Children in the early grades are literal—very literal. Once we establish that one is not to be trusted without the password, most four- to eight-year-olds will rigorously uphold that rule, even if they are talking to their favorite aunt whom they see three times a week. On the other hand, if a person approaches our child with ill will, do we really want the child lingering to discuss passwords at all?

There are several tried and true precautions we can take with young, and even older, children. Though personalized items always please children, they should only be items for the home. Backpacks, umbrellas, sweatshirts, or outerwear should never bear a child's name. It provides an easy "in" for strangers.

Often we tell children to run if a car slows or stops and its occupants want to engage them in conversation, but we forget to tell the children to run in the direction opposite the car's. Reminding children not to take shortcuts or walk in abandoned areas is important, as is pointing out that children walking in groups are not as vulnerable as a child walking alone.

85

Parents of very young children need to be more explicit than, "Never talk to strangers."

Ask your child to describe a stranger. Don't be surprised if she says, "A stranger is a great big gigantic furry thing that roars!" Young children need to know that a stranger is anyone who does not know them from school or home. A teenager, an elderly person, and a peer can all be strangers.

However, once we deal with the issue of strangers, we must face what current research indicates about sexual abuse of children: frequently, relatives or family friends interact inappropriately with children. One of the finer concepts introduced on the subject is that of personal space and trusting one's gut feelings. Children can be guided to trust their feelings. If they feel uncomfortable, they should leave the situation or speak up about their discomfort. Parents must be cautious when training their children to comply with the wishes of adults. Children should be encouraged to say no to an adult when they are not comfortable with the adult's requests.

I think it is important to think about trust and our young children. We cannot become so obsessed with instilling fear that we forget to nurture a sense of trust. We cannot keep our children in a bubble, safe from all the evils of the world. Even if we could, I am not sure we would want to. We need to strike a balance between instilling a sensible fear and encouraging our youngsters to believe in the basic goodness of humankind.

We cannot afford to let the violent acts of some disturbed segments of our society color our perceptions of the entire human race. Children need to be aware of potential danger, but they also need to believe that the world is a good place in which to live, and that we can sometimes rely on the kindness of strangers.

7

Home
for the Holidays

Halloween Celebrations: Getting Trickier Every Year

Last year on Halloween night, three delightful young women presented themselves at my door. Their costumes were of the farmer/scarecrow variety, with straw hats, coveralls, and patches. "Would you like a song or a joke?" the tallest inquired.

Not knowing whether this was a trick or a treat, I politely responded, "Excuse me?"

"We have three very good jokes and one mediocre song," the middle farmer claimed. "Which do you prefer?"

Shortly, the youngest child in the trio laughed with delight at my confusion and said brightly, "We just moved here from Iowa, and in Iowa you always do a song, a dance, or a joke in order to get your treat." I opted for the joke. Though I have relatives in Iowa and had not heard of this custom, I had, indeed, heard all three jokes. I laughed appreciatively, however, as I handed out treats, and they were off to the next house. I hadn't thought of them again until I ripped the September page from my calendar a few weeks ago. There was Halloween, only thirty days away.

I thought—with some annoyance, as most busy parents do—that this is a holiday I could easily live without. Then I thought, as most child development people do, of how easily children are exploited by Halloween and other holidays. Finally, I thought of the three girls from Iowa and their enthusiastic insistence on maintaining their traditional approach to Halloween by sharing it with their New Hampshire neighbors. Children sometimes favor this holiday over Chanukah, Christmas, or even their birthdays.

It is understandable that parents have reservations about Halloween. Crime is up; media coverage is frightening. We hear of terrible tricks delivered by emotionally disturbed adults to the little witches and goblins who venture out on Halloween night. Candies laced with poison and apples with razor blades or common pins inside have become typical evening news for October 31.

We live in a troubled society. Often, those who were abused or threatened as children use this night to experiment with their own deep-seated fears by threatening youngsters who are trick-or-treating unattended. The elderly fear vandalism or abuse from older adolescents.

It's no wonder that governors of several states have suggested a ban on trick-or-treating to local communities. Yet where does this leave the children? It has always been the one day of the year when make-believe and magic are socially acceptable and even encouraged.

For parents, kept busy trying to decide whether to stretch the candy out for weeks or let their children indulge to the limit, and attempting to discard all unwrapped treats without inviting tears, the concerns, aggravations, and fear of cavities seem to outweigh the merits of this evening of fun.

To children, though, it remains a real focus of the year. For young children, dressing up and make-believe are ways of testing their strengths or playing with their fears. A child fearful of her own aggressive feelings can derive a benefit from roaring at others while disguised as a lion. A timid child, costumed as a superhero, can become, for a while, powerful and in control. For older children, who usually spend too much time watching TV or listening to music, dreaming up a disguise can make use of creative energy and ingenuity.

There are several things that parents can do to enhance the celebration of Halloween. Avoid the overpriced and poorly made costumes the discount stores offer. Though your child is bound to plead for various characters, heavily advertised and ready-made, she will be disappointed, in the end, if you buy them. Most packaged costumes are so flimsy that they are torn and ruined before the school party is over—leaving a tired, tearful youngster with nothing to wear for trick-or-treating.

Gather together old clothes, hats, material (that you don't care about!), old sheets, spreads, or curtains. Add some cardboard, masking tape, yarn, markers, a roll of aluminum foil, boxes, brown paper bags, cotton balls, and assorted trims. Provide scissors, glue, and an extra pair of hands. Then let your children create! Have some cider and popcorn on hand and you'll have a pre-Halloween party the children will enjoy as much as the big night.

Do talk about safety with your children. Insist that they bring all treats home for your inspection before eating. Set an example in your neighborhood by offering raisins, pretzels, or small books and toys instead of candy.

One of the things we often overlook is the anticipation/letdown effect so inevitable with celebration. Children talk for weeks at school about who or what they will be for Halloween. They envision endless supplies of treats and the thrill of disguises, masks, and make-believe. Excitement grows as the night approaches. The reality cannot possibly live up to the fantasy evening the children dream of.

In *The Pleasure of Their Company*, Bank Street College suggests that parents provide a "winding down" experience for the children. An after-trick-or-treat party for a small group featuring nourishing food and hot cider or cocoa gives the children a chance to relax, share their experiences, extend the holiday a bit, and unwind.

We tried this last year and it was most successful. The boys each invited two friends. We felt more comfortable sending them down the street in a group of six. We planned favorite foods for the after-party, which made coming home on time a little easier. They shared funny stories and talked about people they'd met in their travels. They dumped out their treats and spent a half-hour trading licorice for Peppermint Patties, peanut butter cups for bubble gum. There was less resistance to ending the evening when everyone had had a chance to relax, visit, and mull over their celebration.

It is important, in light of the frightening stories in recent years surrounding Halloween, that we carefully define safety rules for our children. But it is also important that we reassure them that the world is a good place to be and that we will take an interest in their holiday celebration...even if it isn't one that the adult world cherishes.

A Time for Masking Feelings, Fears, and Fantasies

Outside, brisk breezes scatter bright orange and gold leaves in every direction. This is the time of year that seems to lend itself to the robust activities of children interacting with nature. Every generation takes delight, for a few years, anyway, in the activity of raking huge piles of leaves together to jump in, hide in, or ride a bike through. Children collect acorns and dried leaves and watch squirrels storing up their winter treasures. The mountains turn a blazing orange and the central park is a splash of crimson and gold.

It is the season for disguises and spooks and scary stories. In recent years, many communities have taken the initiative to move the emphasis of the ancient celebration of Halloween from the custom of trick-or-treating back to the celebration of harvest bounty, parades, and entertaining at home. Some of these festivities begin right after Labor Day. Local farms offer hay rides, pony rides, apple picking, pumpkin pies, and even music for those who want to get out in the autumn sunlight.

There is probably wisdom in the decisions of many towns to have Halloween participation based on school or town hall parties and parades. With vandalism, child abuse, and missing children so much in the news, parents have become anxiety-ridden over this tradition of trick-or-treating. Some areas have declared certain hours, during daylight, for children to do their Halloween visiting. Older children complain of these changes, claiming, "It's no fun if it's light out!" or "How can you scare anybody in broad daylight?"

This sometimes makes parents wonder about their children's motives. "Do they want to be scared?" we ask ourselves. Then why do they get upset if they actually are scared or tricked?

For children, part of the joy of this whole Halloween experience is that it provides an opportunity for testing fears and fantasies. They can "act out" in outrageous ways, and on Halloween it's funny or socially acceptable behavior. Ideally, most young children are encouraged at home or in preschool to dress up to play roles and imagine themselves pilots or pirates or lion tamers throughout the year. But often, adults are eager to do away with that make-believe time of childhood, which actually provides a perfect medium for stretching the imagination and trying the world on for size. It's a shame that so often the only opportunity children have to engage in this world of dress-up and fantasy is Halloween.

If Halloween celebrations change from year to year, but continue to encourage children to explore the worlds of make-believe and play-acting, then the important role of the holiday will be preserved. It is this ability to "put on a different face" that provides children with such a rewarding experience. It's the very essence of being someone they are not that gives children such a fascination with this day of dress-up and trickery.

I realized just how much is involved in all this disguising the other day, when I overheard several mothers discussing their children's plans for the big night. One woman was distressed by her daughter's choice for Halloween. "I suggested a robot, a bear, or a clown," she lamented, "but Jennifer insists on being a princess!"

"Well, that may seem too stereotypical for you," her friend offered, "but at least it's easy to come up with! Patrick wants to be a pizza!"

A third mother was amazed that her child, who has a hard time standing up for his rights at preschool, had chosen to be an all-powerful TV action hero.

And so it seems that children will pick and choose either an idea from a commercial, a superhero, a character who epitomizes everything he or she is not, or something (like a princess) that's bound to trigger some kind of response in a parent.

This point was brought home to me just last week. At the end of a long day filled with too many meetings, I paused to discuss the presidential debates with a colleague. We got to reminiscing about the old days, when there was government support for social services. "It's hard times for human services now," my associate stated sadly. "Day care, counseling, and services for battered families have all had such budget cuts that one wonders where it will end."

"I know," I replied. "It's really hard for me to see so many people in need and so much money spent on weapons of war."

In a complete change of subject, my friend suddenly inquired, "Does your twelve-year-old still involve himself in the Halloween festivities?"

"Yes, he does," I said. "It's so funny at these transitional stages...talking about a date for the Halloween dance one minute and a costume for trick-or-treating the next!"

"What's he doing for a costume?" my friend inquired.

I hesitated for a moment, recalling my discussion minutes before; my distress for defense spending levels. "He's going to be some kind of terrorist, I think," I finally admitted reluctantly. I felt compelled to add, somewhat defensively, "All the kids want those camouflage pants and all. I mean, I don't really like it, but at twelve it seems like it's his business."

My friend started laughing appreciatively. "Relax," she said, still laughing, "Michael's going as a warrior. And won't they get a rise out of both of us!"

"Take Joy"

Several brochures have already arrived at my house offering seminars on surviving the holiday season, or "Dealing with Depression in December," sponsored by various mental health agencies, school PTOs, and other groups in service to the community. These provide, no doubt, significant help to families, as it is commonly accepted that the holiday season is responsible for an increase in depression in the general population from November to January.

But as I set to work on this column early in October, I am puzzled by something. For the past several years, I've been watching a growing phenomenon. It began as a small celebration of autumn. It has become a harvest festival attended by thousands of families throughout the weekends of September and October. These festivals are sponsored by apple orchards, PTOs, farms, churches, and nursing homes. The one I am most familiar with is at a local orchard; it has become an annual event for my family.

There are hayrides, clowns, apple picking, musicians, and family sing-alongs. The air is full of wonderful smells: roasting corn, fresh doughnuts, spicy baked apple pies, coffee, and hot cider. Decorations of Indian corn, pumpkins, and cornstalks are a feast for the eyes. It is, quite frankly, intoxicating. Full of glorious autumn leaves, laughing children, and music, it is truly a festival.

Now, I must admit that as my younger children were singing along with the musicians, my teenagers, who were feeding their faces, broke the ecstasy I was feeling with the harsh comment, "Boy! Think of the bucks these guys are raking in!" That was when the parallel struck me. What makes hundreds of people voluntarily participate in a harvest festival, while fearing depression from a winter festival?

It seems that throughout history people have experienced the need to gather together to celebrate life. This celebration has looked similar through the centuries in many ways: food, music, dance, family—enjoyment of the moment. Much of this need for celebration can be met during the winter holiday season. One can focus on the food, friends, and music of this wonderful time of year, or one can grumble about the traffic on the way to Grandma's house, the commercialism that plagues Americans, or how much we are dreading listening to Aunt Mary's litany of aches and pains over the family turkey dinner.

As our children grow, their ability to celebrate life will not be based on the gifts given, or whether the pumpkin pie was homemade or picked up at a bakery on the way home from work. Rather, they will learn to anticipate these events, or dread them from watching and listening to us.

Wise parents have known this through the ages. "No peace lies in the future which is not hidden in this present instant," wrote Fra Giovanni of the holiday season in 1513. "The gloom of the world is but a shadow; behind it, yet within our reach, is joy. Take joy."

Share it with your family. Share it with your friends. Happy holidays.

Home for the Holidays

Oh there's no place like home for the holidays.
No matter how far away you roam
If you long for the sunshine of a friendly gaze
For the holiday, you can't beat home sweet home.

These familiar lyrics evoke the family gathered for Thanksgiving in the Norman Rockwell painting, "Freedom from Want." We all seem to yearn for those fantasy visions of family as the holiday season approaches. My friends all "long for the sunshine of a friendly gaze," but most agree that the home of a friend, not the bosom of the family, is the place to find one.

Leonard's father informs him that if he can't "break that crazy vegetarian fad" to eat his mother's prime rib, he doesn't need to show up.

Ruth dreads the family gathering. Her two-year-old is not up to sharing his toys with his eighteen-month-old cousin. Ruth believes the boys are not old enough to share; her sister feels equally strongly that they should be taught.

Dan knows his mother will greet them after the eight-hour drive with, "It's so good to see you....Oh, my! I see we're still in Pampers." He knows this will create tension between him and his spouse.

Jenny and Mike Stevens believe hitting is not an acceptable way for children to settle differences. Brenda and Bill Stevens believe in "letting the kids battle it out." Usually, the grown brothers are battling verbally about differences in parenting styles by the time Grandma serves the turkey.

What the songs never tell us is the extent of tension that often accompanies the homemade pumpkin pie! This is not to say that shared holiday experiences have to be dismal, tense occasions for extended families. But a realistic look at our family's interactions can help us to tailor our expectations for a reasonable holiday celebration.

The following points might be helpful in making the family gathering more comfortable for everyone involved.

Small children have pretty simple tastes. They may not be interested in cranberry relishes, sage stuffings, creamed onions, or Aunt Kate's special marinated vegetables. Try to focus on the company and conversation. Don't force youngsters to try unfamiliar foods.

Traveling can be as exhausting for children as it is for their parents. Sleeping in strange beds can cause distress in small children, even if they have their own blanket or teddy. Don't be surprised if your child wants you to lie down with her until she falls asleep. This is really a reasonable request if a child is far from home and overtired.

Children who do not see relatives frequently often feel shy, and want and need some distance. Aunt Harriet is old enough to understand that children don't always feel affection for adults they see infrequently. Children shouldn't be forced to hug, kiss, or sit on laps if they are feeling hesitant.

Try to focus on your child's feelings—not on how the extended family views her behavior or your parenting expertise. It is difficult for children when parents have higher expectations than usual because of "what the relatives will think."

Very often, adults like to linger over the holiday meal. It is unfair to expect very young children (or even active sevens and eights!) to sit still for long periods of time. Try to have blocks, Legos, or other engaging activities nearby for little ones to go to when they've had enough of the turkey and its trimmings.

In the case of those delicate issues of children's squabbles and conflicting parenting styles, it's important to remember that we are all different and unlikely to alter each other's behavior by arguing philosophies at family reunions. It is the wise in-law who can step back and say, "You know, you could be right. I'll give that some thought!" Even if you think the comment, criticism, or advice is ridiculous, you can avoid a discussion that, if pursued, will only lead to hurt feelings on all sides.

One of the most difficult things when one returns to the old neighborhood is avoiding the temptation to prove that you are a better spouse, disciplinarian, or parent than anyone else at the gathering. This behavior can often be baffling to youngsters who don't understand why their parents are acting so funny.

One of the very simple facts of life is that it takes two people to have a conflict. If tensions begin to rise because Uncle Fred has had too much to drink, or if the children are getting on Grandmother's nerves, gather your children and some of their cousins and take a brisk walk in the moonlight, or find a quiet spot and read or tell stories to them.

When several generations gather, it is probably impossible to hope for harmony and feelings of good cheer from all. But taking a realistic, flexible attitude about individual differences, and keeping an open mind to the needs and concerns of others, can help families to focus on the festivities and devote less energy to the family flaws.

What Are Your Holiday Traditions?

I was about eight years old when I first had a hunch that the holiday season was not always as joyful for parents as it was for me.

My mother took me shopping for the holidays. The first mall had opened in our town, a suburb of Washington, D.C. Saturdays saw an exodus of station wagons headed for the massive mall with its huge parking areas. We shopped for teachers' gifts, stocking stuffers, and cookie cutters. When we had finished, Mom suggested hot chocolate at the drugstore. There, in a booth by herself, was a friend of my mother's. She was crying and looked exhausted.

Mom joined her immediately. "Good heavens, Berle, what's the matter?" Mom said.

Berle looked up, grateful for a familiar face. "Oh, Anne," she said desperately, "I've lost the car!" Then she burst into tears.

"How could you lose the car, Berle?" mother asked.

Berle sipped tea and sobbed and explained that she'd spent two hours walking around the rows of cars. Now, she said, she couldn't even remember which level she'd come in on. "John will never forgive me," she raved. "I mean, I've misplaced the keys before, but never the car! I just have so much to do...the girls need angel costumes by Wednesday; we have forty people coming for cocktails Friday; I bought stamps for the greeting cards yesterday, and Jimmy licked them all and stuck them on the refrigerator. I spent all afternoon baking gingerbread boys for the school party and the kids ate them when I was in the bathroom. Last summer I bought a bike for Jenny for Christmas and now I can't find it—oh, Anne, I've lost that, too!" And again she burst into tears.

"She's going in circles, Mommy," I said, unaware of my apt description of most mothers at holiday time.

Berle finally found her car, made her costumes, had her party, bought more stamps, and baked more cookies. She probably said, "This was one of the best holidays ever!" when she took the decorations back to the attic in January. But isn't there an easier way?

I'm not sure there is an easy way for families to get through the holiday season. However, at a time when changing family patterns and changing values make it easy to lose traditions, we must make a point of cherishing them for ourselves and for our children. With care and planning, we can help our children to savor the best that the season has to offer, and help them to survive the worst!

Children need traditions. Like adults, they separate the ordinary from the special through celebration. We all savor the first snowfall of winter, the first robin of spring, the lighting of the menorah or Christmas tree. Such occasions are the milestones that mark the seasons and the years in a child's life.

We sometimes forget, when under pressure at this time of year, that children are experiencing pressure of their own: the buildup of excitement, the anticipation, the wondering, the waiting, the living with parents who are more preoccupied than usual, and even the eventual letdown.

But there are things we can do to help. Instead of complaining in front of the children that holiday decorations are up earlier every year, we can comment, "Yes, the holidays are coming, but not for quite a while. It is such a special time that people like to plan ahead. That's why the cards and ribbons are out already." Do plan ahead, but make planning a family affair. Involve the children in your holiday preparations whenever possible. It will reduce the waiting time for children and reduce the workload for parents.

Often we get carried away at this time of year. We get too involved socially; we get overextended financially. We spend too much money on our children and not enough time with them. If we truly want the holidays to have meaning for our families, we should keep things simple and let the children join us in our activities. A bowl full of shiny red apples polished by a three-year-old, popcorn balls made by school-age children, and a holiday nutcracker with mixed nuts can all add a festive air to family celebrations without requiring hours in the kitchen.

If there are treasured recipes to prepare, make it a family affair. Is it Grandma's recipe? Where did she get it? While the cookies bake, family history is being shared. Children love to hear stories of their parents' childhoods—and their grandparents' and their great-grandparents'. Telling family stories of years gone by brings families closer together and connects generations.

Every year at our house, when the tree is decorated, one of the children asks, "Why do we have both a star and an angel on top of our tree?"

And every year we tell the story of our first Christmas in New Hampshire. Newly married and five hundred miles from our families, we decided to splurge on a tree and all the trimmings. Loaded down with boxes of ornaments, lights, and a stand, we were finished...all but the top. "Where are the stars?" my husband inquired of a store clerk.

"What do you mean, stars?" I said. "We've always had an angel!" As the story goes, a tired young man who couldn't cope with people crying and arguing in his store ten minutes before closing on Christmas Eve produced a star with an angel in the middle. To an outsider, it is merely an ornament, probably gaudy. But at our house, it's an heirloom representing a merger of family traditions.

Traditions can be handed down from grandparents, or started this year. The holidays can be a time for passing on a personal commitment to spiritual values held dear for generations, or a celebration of a cultural heritage...rich with fun, food, friends, and family. As Joseph Stein's Tevye reminds us, "Because of our traditions, everyone here knows who he is and why he is here. Without them, our lives would be as shaky as a fiddler on the roof!"

Visions of Sugarplums: Not So Sweet?

It's Christmas Eve. Snow is softly falling. The stockings are hung. The cookies and milk are on the counter with a note to Santa. The children (in matching red flannels for tomorrow's early photos!) fell asleep as Dad read to them from *A Child's Christmas in Wales*. The tree glistens in the corner. Beneath it stretch the piles of gifts that are bound to be opened to shrieks of delight, meeting everyone's desires. Carols play on the stereo. Mom and Dad sip egg nog, toasting the joys of the season.

Early next morning (but not before seven thirty), the household awakens to the patter of little feet. The children are overjoyed. Mom is smiling and serene as the children laugh and play with their new toys. Later, relaxed and cheerful, Dad serves up a six-course meal with fruitcake, plum pudding, and pumpkin pie for dessert. The whole family has gathered for this feast. The in-laws applaud Dad's culinary efforts. All in all, it's a great day for family togetherness and memories.

Each year, when I get my college roommate's photo greeting card, I envision her having this kind of Christmas. Maybe it's the red velvet dresses her daughters wear. Or maybe it's that she lives in New Jersey and we only share the good times when we talk long-distance. Otherwise, the people who live this Christmas fantasy must be somebody else's friends. The people I know are all frantic on Christmas Eve. If they shopped in August, they forgot where they hid the treasures. Or they remember everything...except to take the twenty-four-pound turkey out of the freezer to thaw. So they cry and serve lasagna instead.

The people I know usually drop, exhausted, into bed after assembling toys until two in the morning...only to be awakened at a quarter to six by children insistent on seeing "what we got!" Instead of utterances of joy, our kids say things like, "I told you to tell Aunt Lucy I hate to read and she still sends books!" Or, "So what do they think—I'm a baby? I ask for a CD and they give me Matchbox Cars!" The final comment is often, "Is that all?"

The people I know have children who burp on purpose during the meal for the sheer joy of getting their cousins to laugh and spill their milk. They have fathers-in-law who, when asked to refrain from smoking cigars at the table, say, "So can I go in the kitchen to eat?"

They have sisters who say, "You don't mind exchanging the shirt? I hadn't realized you'd gotten so heavy!" Sometimes my friends wish they could just skip the whole thing.

I read once that on a list of stress-producing stimuli compiled by psychiatrists, Christmas ranked as high as being ten thousand dollars in debt. Most of us have had at least one or two holidays that we'd gladly have traded for a second mortgage! Yet the media continue to push that image of the ideal holiday...and we continue to have vague feelings of disappointment and, like the children, often ask, "Is that all?"

According to psychologists, a major cause of depression during the holidays is the attempt on the part of many of us to live up to the public image of Christmas. We feel the pressure to shop, bake, decorate, and wrap gifts. We write cards, entertain, and rush to holiday concerts at the elementary or high school. We call it a "family time" and spend less time together than usual.

There are ways to have a happier and calmer holiday...if we are willing to take a long look at our traditions and reevaluate their importance. Sometimes traditions outlive their usefulness and become habit. Doing something year after year because it gives us a feeling of comfort and continuity is sharing a deeply-rooted tradition. Doing something year after year because we've always done it and no one wants to admit they no longer enjoy it is to contribute to that feeling of holiday blues that often haunts us.

Changing direction is easier than you might think. Years ago, for instance, when my oldest boys were about four and six, I called the family to the table for Christmas dinner and my son Brian wouldn't come. The silver and crystal sparkled, the bayberry candles were lit. The feast was turkey, of course, with every trimming. "Come on, sweetheart," I urged, "I've made a special dinner and it's getting cold."

Brian stood up, reluctantly. "Gosh, Mom," he said, "when Santa's brung you everything good and they keep playing 'Jingle Bells' and you've already had candy canes...who needs dinner?"

That was the last year a Christmas dinner was cooked at our house. In fact, not having a big meal on Christmas Day is presently one of our holiday traditions. Prior to the big day, we stock up on favorite fruits and nuts, crackers and cheeses, and lots of cider and eggnog. We make trays of raw vegetables and dip ahead of time, and whenever we are hungry, we munch. We savor the quiet informality of our day. Along about New Year's, when the excitement has ebbed and appetites increased, we often cook a turkey. In years to come, as the children mature, a special meal may become an appropriate way to celebrate. For now, the more casual arrangement is best.

Christmas cards are another thing we've cut down on. They had become a chore as well as an ever-increasing expense. So we decided to spend one afternoon making calls to nearby friends to say, "Happy holidays." In the long run, it's no more expensive, less time-consuming, and more emotionally rewarding to actually talk with old friends.

For those of you who use artificial trees and also have storage space, I suggest another time-saver. Though decorating the tree is usually a special ritual for the whole family, assembling it and putting the lights on can be an aggravating task. Why not store it assembled? Large trash bags can cover the branches to prevent dust build-up. Then, in December, just bring it down and plug it in!

In recent years, the statement, "The holidays seem to start earlier every year!" has gotten a lot of bad press. But award-winning composer Jerry Herman addressed this in the song "We Need A Little Christmas," which he wrote for the Broadway musical "Mame." In the play, Auntie Mame is driven to prepare for the holidays even though she knows it is too early in the year. The song goes, "We need a little Christmas, right this very minute....For I've grown a little leaner, grown a little colder, grown a little sadder, grown a little older—yes, we need a little Christmas now."

Most of us recognize in Auntie Mame's song the yearning for gaiety, celebration, and the warmth the holidays promise. The hurried pace that drives most of us through the year seems to demand the reflection encouraged by a quiet snowfall. The music of Christmas is a soothing thing that takes us back to simpler times. We look forward to the holidays. We cherish them. We should reserve the time and energy to thoroughly enjoy them.

Here Comes Santa Claus

Toys R Us is crowded. Through the speaker system, Burl Ives is encouraging me to "Have a Holly Jolly Christmas!" In front of me, a young woman is carrying a baby while pushing a heavily-laden cart down the aisle. Her three-year-old stares with sparkling eyes at the towers of treasures that surround him.

When his hand reaches for a shining tractor, his mother's tired voice snaps, "Timothy, you touch that and Santa won't bring you a thing!" It's an effective threat; Timothy shoves his hands into his pockets and follows his mother down the aisle. I think to myself how hard it is when adults do this to children. It's an easy answer to child discipline for a few weeks. Society endorses it. But it isn't fair to use such tactics on youngsters.

It's confusing for young children when parents read stories like "The Night Before Christmas," which portrays a loving, giving benefactor in Santa, and then sing "Santa Claus is Coming to Town." To adults, the sing-songy verses seem innocent enough: "You'd better not cry. You'd better not pout. I'm telling you why." But for children, the idea that "He sees you when you're sleeping, he knows when you're awake. He knows if you've been bad or good, so be good for goodness' sake" can be frightening.

Children need to be assured that no one knows their secret thoughts. Their joy in the season shouldn't be marred by bribery or a sense that the magic or surprises of the holidays depend on their good behavior. Believing in Santa can be a special part of childhood. But the symbol of Santa should remain a loving, giving figure. He should never be used as a threat or to control children.

When parents are not being tempted to use Santa to help with their child rearing, they are often concerned about their own role in a dishonest plot. "We never lie to her," parents tell me, "but somehow Santa seems like an important part of childhood that we don't want her to miss."

Most experts agree that magic and make-believe are a special feature of childhood that we should aim to preserve. Bruno Bettelheim, in *The Uses of Enchantment*, says, "Children want to think that there's somebody else in the world (besides parents) who does nice things for children."

The question parents worry about most seems to be, "Is the joy of the myth worth the disappointment a child experiences when she discovers the truth?" Experts and school-age children appear to agree that the joy is worth the later disappointment.

When children begin to doubt the jolly old elf, they start asking a lot of questions: How can he get here if it doesn't snow? We always have a fire in the fireplace on Christmas Eve—won't he get burned up? If it takes us half an hour just to get to Aunt Kate's, how can he go all around the world in one night? A good response to these questions is, "Well, what do you think?" If a child wants or needs to keep the story going, she will come up with an adequate answer. If a child continues to push, it's best to be honest.

At least once every holiday season, I reread Virginia O'Hanlon's 1897 letter to the *New York Sun*, and the *Sun*'s editorial response. I am always encouraged by the words, "...Your little friends are wrong. They have been affected by the skepticism of a skeptical age." Some things never change.

Light Up the Darkness

My son Thomas has never complained about his child care provider. Like most young children, he occasionally says, "I wish you did not go to work. I wish we always just stayed home to play." But usually he goes to school and then to child care...and often greets me with, "You're here too soon; I'm still busy!" when I pick him up.

When the clocks were set back a few weeks ago, though, the days seemed much longer to Thomas. "It's hard to wait for you when the dark comes," he said one day. "Will you pick me up when it's light?" he asked another time.

So one day, as I drove to work, I thought a lot about this issue of darkness and light. As winter brings a close to the year, we all sense the darkness, the cold, the need for warmth and brightness. No wonder we have had, for centuries, celebrations that ward off the darkness. It is understandable that we wait in anticipation for the lighting of the menorah or Christmas tree.

There has been much in print in recent years about the materialism that has infiltrated the holiday season. Jewish parents are appalled when their offspring have a Christmas tree sparkling in the corner. They urge their children to teach their grandchildren the true meaning of the holidays—not to compromise by buying into Christmas celebrations.

Christian families often complain that the true meaning of Christmas has been lost to the marketplace. What so many parents forget when celebrating winter holidays is that religious or family traditions of depth are lost on little children, anyway. It is only the spirit we bring to these winter days that leaves a lasting impression on our children.

When our oldest child was very young, we explained to him, at Christmastime, the story of Baby Jesus being born in Bethlehem. We showed him the figures of a crèche (built by my grandfather), which were set up in a special place for the holidays. We congratulated ourselves on our son's reverent response to the true meaning of Christmas.

In January, when a friend stopped by to tell us of her ski trip to Bethlehem, New Hampshire, our son stared as she spoke of snow and winter vacations. "Did you see the Christs?" Sean finally said.

Surprised, we all turned to him. "The Christs?" our friend asked.

"Yes," Sean said, "Mary and Joseph Christ. They live in a barn with many animals." Fortunately, we all had the presence of mind to respond appropriately to Sean's inquiry. But it taught us about the inability of the very young child to put historic things in context. The "spirit" of the holidays is the most that any parents can hope to share with their children at this special time of year.

We are fortunate to share the celebration of Chanukah each year with good friends. For my children, it is a regular part of the winter holiday season. Recently I bought small bags of gold-wrapped coins (Chanukah geld) to have on hand for the holidays. My youngest son was with me in the store. "Is Chanukah coming soon?" he asked. Without waiting for an answer, he launched into a monologue about how many potato pancakes he would eat and how he would play with his dreidel. A stranger listening to this excited speech smiled at Thomas and then at me.

"Your holidays are early this year, aren't they?" she asked.

"Chanukah is soon, right after Thanksgiving," my son told her, "and I can eat all those gold coins, but Santa will probably bring me more for Christmas!"

The woman looked confused, said, "That's nice, dear," and left the store.

At our house, we are not confused by the celebration of two different winter holidays. Chanukah is not Christmas. Christmas is not Chanukah. Both, however, fill that universal need to light a candle in the darkness as the year draws to a close. For our children, it is the respect and reverence for many cultures and traditions that will make a lasting impression. So as the darkness of winter approaches, let's reach out and light a candle for the children. Whether that candle burns on a Christmas tree or in a menorah, let it provide warmth and light for future generations as the darkness comes.

8

Together Times

The Family That Plays Together
—Can Sometimes Be Miserable

Nothing is so frustrating for parents as when well-laid (and sometimes well-paid-for) plans for summer fun end in shouting contests over who gets the seat by the window or who took whose piece of pizza without asking.

Nothing is so frustrating for youngsters as spending a normal day of fun—including some fights over pizza and windows—and feeling that you've really disappointed your parents, although you're not sure just how you did it.

Vacations and specially-planned days of fun sometimes have a way of getting on everyone's nerves. So often we hear ourselves saying, "The more I do for these kids, the less they appreciate." I have a friend who has spent the better part of the last ten years offering exciting trips and experiences to her daughters. Yet she always comes home feeling that it didn't quite meet everyone's expectations.

The problem with expectations is their varied and personal nature. For instance, I once admired a leather-bound edition of Emily Dickinson on a friend's table. "My husband gave it to me," she said without enthusiasm.

"What a treasure," I beamed.

"Not really," she responded, "I hate poetry!" Often we give what it is we would like to receive, and then don't understand when the recipient of our devotion is not delighted.

When planning family days, parents sometimes work with each other without consulting the kids in designing a day they are sure will please the children. Then we feel hurt or angry when the kids don't act totally thrilled with their outing. We might think a day at an art museum and dinner at a nice restaurant is a treat, while our ten-year-old would prefer a roller rink and Pizza Hut. Or, as is often the case at my house, one child votes for history and the other votes for exercise! What is a family to do?

"Togetherness" can be overdone. Though it's always special to find an event that pleases everyone, there is not much point in forcing a sports enthusiast to attend the theater, or vice-versa, in order to make it a family affair.

Children love the individual attention of an adult. Why not go to the theater now with the drama critic and to a ball game later with the Little Leaguer? Sometimes, all our children really want is the pleasure of our company: a walk, an ice cream cone—some time alone together.

Ask the children to do some planning. Or take turns deciding on a location for a day trip. Encourage each family member to be honest about her response to an idea. This saves time, money, and hurt feelings. If you know in advance that your son isn't interested in baseball and you insist on Fenway Park anyway, at least you won't be disillusioned by your child's reaction.

I have been known to force my children to view exhibits or attend concerts from time to time against their wishes. Often when I insist on broadening their cultural horizons, they admit they're glad they went. Other times they tell me they'd rather have spent the time sleeping. You spend your money...you take your chances! But I must admit it's hard to remember a trip that's been considered a total loss...at least by the two who get the seats by the windows!

"He's Taking All the Air-Conditioning!"

When discussing fear of flying recently with a friend, I admitted that there was a time when I, too, shared that phobia. "How did you get over it?" my friend inquired.

"Taking twelve-hour trips in a car with three kids!" was my response.

Anyone who travels with children knows the most common complaints: "Are we there yet?" "I have to go to the bathroom!" "It is, too, my turn to sit by the window." "His foot is on my side of the car!" "He's looking at me bad!"

Is there a way to take a pleasant family vacation that requires hours of driving, eating fast food, and sleeping in motels without feeling, at the end, like you'll never do it again? I think maybe not. Though we have been doing this for years, it always leaves me feeling somewhat drained and wondering if there isn't an easier way.

After a recent car trip during which my three children filled the silence with the usual sibling complaints—"He's taking all of the air-conditioning!" "I don't care if he hates pizza; he picked the breakfast place and I want to go to Pizza Hut for lunch!"—we arrived home exhausted, only to note the boys deeply engrossed in a game of pocket trivia (purchased for the long car trip!) that went on peacefully for about an hour after our return. "Why couldn't you guys have done this in the car?" my spouse foolishly inquired. My thirteen-year-old gave him an incredulous stare and said, "Oh, Dad, you know...cars are for fighting in!"

So it is with this bias that I approach the issue of traveling with children. It isn't easy. Having accepted that fact, it isn't quite so hard to face the inevitable. There are some things we can do to make this time together more rewarding.

Planning ahead is critical when traveling with children. If possible, describe to the children the places they will go, the things they will see. Read books about your destination. Explain to children the changes in their routine schedule. Children are far less likely to balk at things when they know in advance what to expect.

Remember that sleeping away from home can be difficult for young children. Try to be patient and maintain your sense of humor. Remember to bring special blankets or stuffed toys that are comfort items to your child. If a child is really uncomfortable with the alternative sleeping arrangements at a motel or relative's home, everyone might get more sleep if you let the child crawl in with you (rather than try to convince the child that she can sleep without a night light just this once, or that the exposed pipes on the ceiling of Grammy's rec room really aren't snakes!).

Children need to move. One of the reasons we encounter so much bickering among siblings in the back of the car is that children find it hard to sit in one place for a long period. For this reason, even though you may add time to your trip, it is well worth it to stop occasionally at a park or playground to let everyone stretch their legs and move around a bit.

Another thing that definitely affects the behavior of children is what they eat. It is too easy, when away from home, to forget about the effect of nutrition on the way we feel and function. Peanuts, raisins, granola bars, cheese, and crackers are all pretty easy car snacks which provide nourishment and energy essential to getting through the day. Candy, gum, and soda give you something to put in your mouth, but do not provide needed nourishment.

Packing for a long trip can be taxing. If you are traveling into unknown territory, it's a good idea to check on weather reports and to anticipate all possible weather conditions. It's best to pack for both warm and cool temperatures, and always wise to bring rainwear and umbrellas.

A small first aid kit should be in the glove compartment at all times. For long trips, however, you may want to pack an extra bag with cures for the indigestion, diarrhea, constipation, and car sickness that often plague youngsters on long trips. We always bring lotions for sunburn, bug bites, and poison ivy...just in case.

Lastly, there is the bag of activities to keep children distracted and amused as the miles pass. We have found drawing tables and markers to be successful, as well as "pocket" games (where you try to roll little balls into a particular space, and the like). There are magnetic checkers and chess specially designed for travel use. There are even books on travel games to play with your child.

But in the last analysis, there is no way to prevent the "When are we gonna get there?!" And unless you have a single child who gets both back windows, I don't think there's a way to prevent the sibling hassles that seem to be as much a part of the travel experience as paying tolls. But somehow, when you accept this, it becomes easier to deal with. And if you're lucky, like we were, the kids may engage in the pocket games when you get home and leave you in peace while you unload the car!

Making Allowances

If you're a person who likes to "stir the stink," walk into a room full of parents and bring up the subject of allowance. It's a topic everyone has strong feelings about. Few agree on a best policy. Arguments fly.

"Why should I pay my own kids to shovel the walk?"

"I give them everything they need—helping out is part of being a family."

"Maybe so, but if you give them everything they need, how will they learn the value of a dollar?"

Current surveys indicate 85 percent of youths receiving allowances are expected to do chores—or no allowance! By binding household chores and allowance together, we guarantee certain problems for ourselves and our children. With this program, if a child decides to live without the allowance, she feels free to leave chores undone.

We end up with two problems. We need help, and we want our children to be experienced in money matters. If we withhold allowance, our children will remain inept at handling money. The only way kids can learn about money is to have some. Parents and children should agree on the amount, depending on the child's age, expenses, and family resources. In order for children to actually learn money management, this sum must be regularly delivered and not withdrawn as punishment. It should be one of the benefits of family living, just as sharing household tasks should be one of the responsibilities of family living.

Once we give the child her allowance, how it is spent should be up to her. If we forbid her to purchase something because it is poorly made, we deny her the chance to learn this lesson for herself. Parents have to be realistic about errors in judgment, which are inevitable. It takes a long time and a few mistakes to develop money sense.

A publication which can help your child make informed decisions in money matters is _Zillions_ (published by Consumer Reports). This monthly magazine offers tips on buying toys and clothes, gives money-saving suggestions, and points out the fallacy in much of the TV advertising directed at youngsters.

Adults often complain that children don't appreciate what they have, or don't understand the value of money. Yet most of us forget to provide real learning opportunities in this area. Giving children an allowance, no strings attached, is the first step. Being patient with the inexperienced spender is next. Holding back on the "I told you so" when your child's poor investment falls apart is important. In most cases, extending credit to youngsters is not a good idea. If a twelve-year-old spends all of her allowance on tapes, then wants an advance on next week's when a friend calls and wants to go to the movies, the loan should be denied. We defeat the budget-learning process if we extend credit on this basis.

In addition to offering a regular allowance to children, there are several things we can do to encourage growth of financial competence. Offer salary for extra jobs, such as baby-sitting, cleaning the garage, and shoveling snow. (Not to be confused with emptying trash, making beds, doing dishes, or other regular household tasks which children should routinely share with parents.) Offer savings incentives to children. Once a month or yearly (with older children), match their savings. Talk with your kids about the costs of operating a car, shopping for groceries, and providing heat and electricity.

An eight-year-old friend of mine used to have "eyes bigger than her stomach." Her parents frequently complained that she would insist on ordering expensive items at a restaurant and then eat only half. Her parents would get angry; she would feel guilty. Finally, the family voted on a new policy. Noelle may order whatever she likes. If she eats it, Mom and Dad pay. If she doesn't, Noelle pays.

Recently, we ate at a restaurant offering tasty after-dinner treats, in huge portions. While her mother and I talked, Noelle summoned the waiter. "Excuse me," she inquired. "Can you order half of one of those desserts?" She's thought a lot lately about consuming and spending!

Sharing the Workload

In about a month, my family will begin what we refer to as Hell Week—that time when the house receives a cleaning and overhaul from top to bottom. We will make endless lists of what needs to be done: easy jobs, hard jobs, messy jobs, time-consuming jobs and the ones that everyone hates to do. We'll all choose from each of the above categories. We'll complain a bit, laugh a bit, sweat a lot. But then it will be done and we'll all feel good about it. It's as easy as that. Right?

Wrong! It's a system better than some we've tried and one developed after many years of negotiating, contracting, discussing—and shouting and pouting, too.

People who live together should share the workload. It sounds simple enough and it's true. Unfortunately, the whole area of work and who should do it is surrounded by myths, sexist conditioning, and outmoded authoritarian practices on the part of parents.

Children have a genuine sense of fairness and a real interest in work. Often, when they resist doing chores, it's not the work they are rebelling against but the way in which it is approached. Too often we order children to do something and tell them when to do it rather than asking for their help and mapping out a time frame in which the task needs to be done.

The first mistake parents often make is refusing the help of the very young child because they think, "It's easier to do it myself." We are all guilty of racing through work while our children sleep at night, attend school, or are involved outside, because we can get more done in those times. But to continually deny a child the opportunity to work because she can't do a complete or competent job is to rob her of an important step in developing independence. It's of greater importance that your two-year-old unloads groceries than that boxes be put on one shelf and canned goods on another.

Last year, our silverware drawer was always a jumble of utensils: for our three-year-old, it was a real challenge to get the things from the dishwasher to the drawer. Now it is fun to put all the spoons in one section and forks in another. But if, when he was three, we had insisted on things being in their proper places, his interest would have faded completely.

Families who sit down together and discuss what needs to be done and who's going to do it tend to get more accomplished and have fewer martyrs than families who randomly stab at household chores. When children share in the decision-making process and agree to a list of policies, they are more willing to work and less likely to balk over their share of the responsibility.

A sample contract of "Household Work Rules" might be:

- Laundry will be done only if it makes it to the hamper. Parents agree not to harp about clothes on the bedroom floor. Children agree not to blame parents if they left a uniform in a heap on the floor and it's not ready for the game on Saturday.
- Toys will be picked up before bedtime. Parents reserve the right to pick up anything left behind, but will not accept responsibility for remembering where they put unclaimed items.
- Groceries will be marked on a shopping list by the person who eats the last granola bar, uses the last Kleenex, finishes the box of cereal, etc. If anyone forgets, the person who shops will not know to buy granola bars and everyone will be without.

It is necessary for families to recognize and deal with stereotypical approaches to household chores. It is unfair for daughters to set and clear the table every night, while sons shovel snow whenever there's a storm. It's unfair for sons to trim bushes, mow lawns, and plant gardens, fighting heat, humidity, or mayflies, while daughters dust tables, sheltered from the elements. Some kind of rotation of tasks is a better approach.

Teenagers employed outside of the home should still do their share of household chores. Housework will always be with all of us. Whatever jobs or activities we pursue outside of the home, our responsibility to shared labor within the home remains the same.

We all know what fair is. Four hours spent parenting at the movies and Pizza Hut does not equal four hours parenting in the middle of the night with a sick child. Washing the car on the weekend does not equal washing dishes or laundry every day.

Children are great (better than most parents) at determining what a fair workload is for everyone. Talk with them. Make lists. Draw up a contract. It really works...and before you know it, so does the whole family.

The Picture-Perfect Family

My friend Ann is always hounding me to share "unprintable" stories. "Families need to hear from a professional that the kinds of crazy things that go on in their own homes are okay," Ann says, "and nobody tops the Mooneys for crazy stories."

We had this discussion again when I was complaining that I had just paid the dry cleaners to wash, starch, and hang a ripped, bleached-out Aerosmith T-shirt. "Lovely," the clerk said with a hint of a question mark in her tone, as she handed me this treasure with the rest of the week's shirts and blouses. Feeling a bit foolish, I decided to make no comment at all. I did make a mental note to charge the one who had dropped it into the wrong dirty clothes pile for the laundry fees, but I couldn't help wondering, as I drove home, how it is that some families keep their systems running so smoothly, while ours chugs along choppily, occasionally breaking down completely.

"People lie!" Ann says flatly. "Show me a couple that doesn't fight and I'll show you a couple of liars or a couple of corpses!" Maybe she's right.

In the front hall of my home hang two very impressive portraits: one of the entire Garhart clan, the other of the entire Mooney clan. Both were taken on the same June afternoon eight years ago. My sister's Virginia acreage was blossoming to perfection. You would never guess from the scrubbed, smiling faces the photographer caught that it was ninety-eight degrees in the shade with 91 percent humidity. Visitors often comment on the portraits and say how wonderful it must be to be part of such a grand extended family group. I am always somewhat amused by this, as the portraits continue to represent to us the longest running cold war of this twenty-year union.

It's a story that's been shared only with intimates until now. But Ann is right: "the family," "family reunions," "family vacations," "a typical happy American family"—all these phrases conjure up visions that make our own family group grow pale or even seem defective. Raised on stories concluding, "They got married and lived happily ever after," we are often unprepared for the "worse" we claimed we would take along with the "better."

That reunion, for my family, embodied the worst of all the issues family therapists tell us will make or break a marriage. Money was a big problem that year. We were settling into a new house and hadn't sold the old one yet. "We can't take the station wagon to Virginia," David stated emphatically a week before the reunion. "The gas will cost too much and you'll want the air-conditioning on and it's out of the question. Pack only two suitcases. We don't need many clothes—we haven't got the funds to go anywhere, anyway."

For those of you who don't know what a Dodge Omni looks like, it resembles a golf cart but supposedly seats five. By the time the five of us, two suitcases, and a large box of Pampers were packed into the Omni, I was feeling so cool toward my spouse that I probably didn't need the air conditioner, anyway.

It was a long trip—twelve hours, counting a dinner stop. When we arrived at my sister's house, the evening air had cooled to about eighty-five degrees. The house was about ninety-two. Now, I've known my sister my whole life. Our housekeeping standards are different. So why did I get so angry when I had to shovel a path to the bed, take storm windows off it, and put sheets on it before I could fall into it? We were not off to a good start.

The Carol/David unit was the only one that laid claim to both tribes arriving that morning. The Garharts were dressing up for the portraits. The Mooneys were dressing down. The potato chips and cookies were melting together before ten.

Every family has its characters. Roles are acted out; unpleasant patterns are reinforced. After I insisted that the Garhart photos be taken first so that my three children could look good for the dressed-up portraits, my brother, the last sibling, was nowhere to be found. His father fussed and fumed and insisted on searching the town for him. When Ben finally arrived, we had to wait another half-hour for Dad to get back.

On the Mooney side, blood pressures were rising as the meal was held up by the tardy Ben. The Mooneys always eat early. The Garharts always eat late. The photographer tried to be polite.

The Mooney brother known as a tightwad tried to drink a beer. Earlier in the day, when everyone had thrown money into the pot for liquid refreshments, Alan had declined to contribute. "We won't drink any," he said. As temperatures rose, his sister Kate made sure he didn't.

"I've never seen such a selfish family in my life!" Alan's wife shouted at his sister. "When my family has a reunion, the adults pay for everything."

Without attempting tact, my spouse said flatly, "We *are* the adults." So Molly left in a huff and returned with a cheap jug of wine that she shared with no one.

My spouse had just spent a year as the primary parent to our three children. He had put dinner on the table, done laundry, and typed my term papers as I finished graduate school. He'd put in hours walking the floor with the baby as teeth erupted. Now, in the company of his macho brothers, he was making "Home Improvement"'s Tim Taylor look sensitive. As the women put food on the table and amused the large group of children, the Mooney Boys drank beer, told jokes, and suggested to wives that the baby seemed to need a new diaper.

Rage was building in my heart. I wondered if my old boyfriend from college still lived in Fairfax...and was he still single? I wondered what had made David seem so attractive years before—how could I have made such a mistake?

The weekend finally ended and we silently filed back into the Omni and headed for New Hampshire. Family relationships were now competing with the war in the Middle East. There had been no time or privacy for communication. David was not sure why I was so mad. I was not sure why I was married.

The children, unaccustomed to this big a chill, were quiet, too. I read my book and pretended I didn't know any of them. As the sun beat down on our un-air-conditioned car, traffic moved slowly. Roadwork kept the expressway moving at an in-town rate. Finally the boys started in.

"Mom." I ignored them.

"Dad, we've got a problem back here with the baby."

"Solve it," David responded curtly.

"Here, Mom, take this."

Annoyed, I held my open hand toward the backseat. No realistic approach to family living could have prepared me for the pile of poop my young son placed in my hand. I stared in amazement, holding the treasure too close to David's face. (I later reminded him that, had we taken the more spacious station wagon, it wouldn't have seemed threatening, or at least it would have been farther from his face.)

"Shit!" I shouted in indignation, though all weekend I'd been telling my teenage brothers that that was inappropriate language to use in front of my young children.

"Exactly," David countered dryly.

Too stunned for quick action, I sat holding this load in space and wondering how my dream of rearing a big, happy family had been reduced to this. "Will you get rid of that?" David glared impatiently. Angrily, I pitched the load out the open window.

Perhaps if the day hadn't been so hot and still, it wouldn't have happened. Perhaps if roadwork hadn't forced the traffic to slow, it wouldn't have happened. Perhaps if the car had been a brown station wagon instead of a white Porsche, it wouldn't have mattered. It was the hysteria in the backseat that brought our attention to the landing. The boys knelt, looking back at the remains of our crisis, splattered on the low white hood of the car behind us.

My face flamed. I was horrified. I would not look at the young couple who stared out in bewilderment from their shiny sports car. "Did they see me do that?" I asked David, forgetting that we were not speaking. David, who is not as quick as I to worry about what people think, was feeling some stress.

"How should I know," he sputtered through clenched teeth.

"Maybe they'll think it was a bird," I said. David, who often says my mental ability was what first attracted him to me, stared at me in disbelief. I recognized the look on his face. I'd worn it myself when he was doing his Archie Bunker act. I knew he was wondering if his old girlfriend still lived in Alexandria, and was she still single?

We both started to laugh. "This is the lowest moment of my life," I said dramatically.

"Oh, come on," David chided with his usual it-could-be-worse routine. "It could have been a convertible," he said calmly, and headed for the exit ramp.

How Old Is Old Enough?

All week I've been interviewing parents and small children who are about to make the big transition from home to group child care. The process is life and separation, on a smaller scale. There is three-year-old Heather, who booms in ready to take the world by the tail. She joins every group, laughs with the children, and makes herself at home at once. There is Chad, who clings to his mom the entire visit. He wants to be carried, does not want to see what the school has to offer, and hides his face each time a child approaches. And there is Aaron, who insists he wants to stay with the kids when his mom and I head for the office—but pops in to check on us every six minutes or so.

I see the struggle each parent and child experiences as he or she prepares for this initial separation. Heather's mom is worried that Heather will make herself "too much at home"; Chad's parents are afraid he might be sad and lonely, and have a hard time adjusting. Aaron's parents see that he's unsure, which makes them feel the same way.

For parents and children, there is a lifetime of juggling dependence and independence. When is it time to hold on; when to let go? How old is old enough to go downtown alone, sleep over, stay without a baby-sitter? How old is too old for blankies and bottles and thumbs, and what do we do instead?

Grandparents can often recount for us, after forty years, the exact flavor of the evening when a son or daughter first had the car for the night, or traveled alone.

I remember the first time my oldest boys went off for the day with people we didn't know very well. A friend from our son's kindergarten class asked both boys to go to Edaville Railroad in Massachusetts. They were supposed to return at seven. By eight o'clock I was pacing the floor impatiently, by nine I was worried sick, and when they arrived at 10 P.M., I had already called the police, the hospitals, and my mother, so she could calm me down. As I cried, long distance, she retold every story of my brothers, my sister, and me being lost, late, or on our own—and how we always came back. I had almost started to laugh again when the boys walked in, all excited about their adventure. Mr. Dube, the friend's father, had gotten lost in Boston and they couldn't find their way out.

"We weren't scared, though," Brian boasted. "Mr. Dube acts just like Mom when she doesn't know where she's going...says the same words and every-thing! So we felt kind of at home."

Over the years my tolerance grew, my panic lessened, and I adjusted somewhat to the routine separations that help both parents and children to grow. But there were still those harrowing times, like letting Brian go to Disney World with a group, letting Sean fly airplanes, and, last summer, letting Tom go fishing with a friend but no grown-ups.

A big moment came last week when my neighbor's daughter, Emily, called and wanted to know if Erin, my youngest child—not quite three—could come over to play. I asked Emily if I could speak to her mom. "We were just on our way to day care," I told my friend Cindy. "I really need to be there for the afternoon shift today."

Cindy laughed warmly and said, "Well, we weren't asking *you* over to play!"

"Oh!" I said, caught short by this new turn of events. "I'm not sure if Erin understands that I'm not coming for coffee." Those are the conditions under which Erin and Emily usually see each other.

"Give it a try!" Cindy said. "I'll call if she has a problem."

So I drove down the street and stopped at my neighbor's house. But before I was out of the car, Erin had unbuckled her seat belt, opened the car door, and run across the yard to Emily. "Bye, Mom," she shouted enthusiastically, leaving me alone on the sidewalk with a big lump in my throat.

I got back in the car. The radio was playing that old sixties tune, "Turn, Turn, Turn." "To everything there is a season..." A time for holding on and a time for letting go. For me, that time has come once again. As I drove away, I saw in the rearview mirror my big girl...deeply involved in play with her friend.

Those Taxing, Troublesome, Trying, but Terrific Teens

For about six months now, every time the issues of curfew, allowance, or bedtime have come up at our house, our oldest son has had the same input: "I'm almost a teenager, you know." This is always spoken in a tone which implies that being a teenager should have dramatic impact on curfews, allowances, or bedtimes.

It occurs to me suddenly that we should have "pre-adolescence" classes for parents, the way we have prenatal and childbirth classes. I should have prepared for this. I should have seen it coming. The signs were all there.

Years ago, getting this child to brush his hair once a day was a challenge. Now, availability of hot water is declining while shampoo consumption is on the rise. And how the hair looks can make or break an otherwise fine day.

Then there was the day when the suggestion to recopy an assignment brought an outburst of anger and frustration. Two hours later, the work done, my son walked in with a satisfied smile and apologized for his temper. "I don't know what hit me," he said, looking genuinely confused. "It just seemed like an impossible task at the time, and I felt so mad, I could burst. Now it seems silly that I got so upset."

Though these indications should have set me thinking, it wasn't until the day we were discussing prison reforms after a television special on the subject that I began to face the fact that I am living with an adolescent son. Our conversation went something like this:

Sean: What do you think of all those TVs and pool tables in prisons, Mom?
Me: I'm not sure what you mean.
Sean: Society shouldn't pay for recreation facilities for robbers and murderers.
Me: What do you think they should do?
Sean: They oughta sit and look at the walls like in the scene where you kept saying, "Isn't it awful?"
Me: You mean the place with the rats?
Sean: Yeah—you don't want to live with rats, you shouldn't act like one.
Me: I can't help but think that that kind of life won't help anyone to live better in society.

Sean: Well, you're wrong, Mom. You used to make a lot of sense, but lately when we talk I can't believe some of the things you say. You have changed a lot lately. Sometimes you're like a different person.

CLICK! That one got through to me.

Our "almost" teenager recently turned thirteen. Though we have our ups and downs, most days are good. It seems to me that the "terrors of teenagers," like the "terrible twos," get too much press. There are so many delightful aspects of life with teenagers. It's nice to come home after working late and find a fire started or a salad made...even if it is accompanied by a sheepish grin and, "I have this term paper I was hoping you could type!"

It's exciting to have an actual exchange of ideas. It can also be somewhat threatening when your child's political or social commentaries are contrary to everything he's heard at home. The tip for parents, at this point, is to understand the adolescent's need to separate from us. They need and savor their independence. And since they are and will continue to be financially dependent on us for some time to come, ideas and opinions are the realm in which most teenagers assert themselves. It's important for parents to cultivate a tolerance for a wide range of behaviors and attitudes, though we might be uncomfortable with some of them.

Fran Lebowitz, in *Social Studies*, offers this advice to teenagers: "Should your political opinions be at extreme variance with those of your parents, keep in mind that while it is indeed your constitutional right to express these sentiments verbally, it is unseemly to do so with your mouth full—particularly when it is full of the oppressor's standing rib roast."

For many adolescents, proving their intellectual superiority to their parents is a necessary step toward separating from them and developing a strong personal identity. The last thing these youngsters need is for parents to prove that we, indeed, are older, wiser, and more experienced. Our children are well aware of this, even if unwilling to admit it.

The key to successful parenting in these years is establishing a good balance between guiding and letting go. Learning to respect a teenager's need for privacy while still being in touch with her needs is a tricky job. For years, our children need so much from us that it is often difficult to stand back when the time comes and let them take responsibility for themselves. It's a time to reexamine household rules. Do they continue to make as much sense for a fourteen-year-old as they did for a ten-year-old? Or are we strictly enforcing dated regulations because we fear change or loss of control?

Though the teenage years are a time when our children need our support and presence perhaps more than ever, it is also a time for parents to listen, strive for flexibility, and hold on to a sense of humor. We need to have faith in the values and parenting we have provided for our offspring in their early years and trust that they will go on from here, feeling good about themselves. We need to expect their mistakes as they try to find a place for themselves in the scheme of things. And when they take their tumbles, we can try to be nearby to help them sort out the pieces as they put themselves back together.

There is too much of a tendency to highlight the problems we encounter as we struggle in our roles as parents. We forget to focus also on the positive aspects of watching children grow.

On my son's thirteenth birthday, we took a few of his close friends to a movie and out to eat. Though we sat at a nearby table, we couldn't help but hear and be amazed by the conversation, sharpness of wit, and exuberance for life this group of friends shares.

"Haven't they all grown into real fine company?" my husband commented when we returned home.

"Yes, they really have," I agreed. "Though it's funny to look up when I talk to them."

"Well, at least we don't have to listen to 'I'm almost a teenager' anymore!" we said simultaneously.

Before we stopped laughing, our eleven-year-old joined us. "That was a good day," he said. "Can I do that for my thirteenth?"

"You've got a long time to worry about that," I responded.

"Not really," he said emphatically. "I really am almost a teenager, you know."

9

Perspectives on Parenting

"What Kind of Horrible Mother Am I, Anyway?"

"I'm just not a natural-born mother," my sister-in-law sobbed into the phone. "I always thought I would be a good mother, that I'd love it, that it would make me happy..." At that, her voice broke and she began to cry again. In the background, I could hear my six-week-old nephew wailing, too. It was eleven thirty at night, an hour when most people are sleeping. I was wishing I was one of them. Yet I was aware of how important it was for my sister-in-law to have a listener, another mother. It is a hard time for women when the moment of truth arrives, when the reality of motherhood is seen as painfully separate from the myth, the fantasies, the "...and they got married and lived happily ever after" fairy tales.

Though seventeen years have passed since I first faced that moment, I can easily conjure up the exact feelings I had. Initially, it was disappointment, that is-this-all-there-is? feeling that comes when a much-anticipated event turns out to be ordinary or, even worse, awful. For many of us, the idea that true fulfillment as a woman comes with giving birth and raising children has deeply penetrated our consciousness. The reality of doing it could never compare to the image of mothering we fabricate for ourselves.

After my disillusionment came a horrible feeling of shame. What would people think if I said the baby is driving me crazy? Why can't I feel maternal, like mothers are supposed to? How can I get mad at such a tiny, helpless little being? What kind of a horrible mother am I, anyway?

I remember working up the courage to share a few of my concerns with another young mother in my neighborhood. "Sometimes I find it so hard," I confided. "I miss work. I feel inadequate when the baby cries and I can't get him to stop. I'm tired a lot. It's not quite the way I had hoped it would be." My friend set down her coffee mug, looked at me thoughtfully for a moment or two, then donned a bright smile and said, "It must be awful to feel like that, but I wouldn't know. My baby is just the answer to my dreams. I love being a mother." Then she hopped up to make more coffee and flip on the TV. End of discussion.

Now I was glad my sister-in-law had me on the other end of the phone. At least I could keep her from thinking she was the only mother with these feelings. "Maryanne," I started carefully, "no one is a natural-born mother. I've worked with children and parents for years, and I've yet to meet a 'natural-born mother.' It's hard—especially if you think it's not going to be. I would worry about you if you just loved having your sleep interrupted every few hours. There is nothing fun about walking the floor with a screaming baby. The responsibility is constant and overwhelming. Your job is to adjust to these stresses, not to enjoy them. No one enjoys this part of parenting."

Most parents who have spent years living with children can talk about the deep joy that this job has brought to their lives. The problem is that, at the beginning, one doesn't really have those positive experiences stacked up to weigh against the hard parts. So it is tough to see beyond the stresses of the moment.

My one-year-old daughter is really a challenge these days. Friends say, "Boy, she is really a mover!" Neighbors say, "She's a charmer, but she never stops!" Strangers say, "Why, she must have just gotten up from a long nap."

"No," I usually respond. "She's always like this." Sometimes, I'm sure, the strangers pick up on the fatigue in my voice. I'm tired a lot. There are days when I have a hard time dealing with this toddler's antics.

On one such day last week, my seventeen-year-old son came in from school and asked brightly, "How was your day?"

"It stunk," I replied emphatically. "Your sister hasn't slept all day. She dumped the spider plant. She screamed through the last few aisles at the supermarket. She put bananas all over her head right after her bath. Need I say more?"

"Having a few regrets, Mom?" he asked directly.

"No," I said impatiently. "I'm just having a hard day—it comes with the job. But today I'm not liking it very much." And at that moment I realized that the benefit of experience in this job is that you know how quickly change comes to growing youngsters. You know that rough stages are replaced by more placid ones—which, in turn, are replaced by even rougher ones. But, all in all, the childhood years are brief. You become less eager to hurry the experience.

This is not to say that seasoned parents enjoy or even cope with the hard times any better. The difference is sometimes as slight as saying, "My day stunk," rather than, "My job stinks," or "I stink at doing this job." This is the perspective I've been trying to share with my sister-in-law as she travels this rough terrain for the first time.

It's been a rough week at our house. One son is furious with us because he's doing poorly in math and possibly faces summer school. "Why didn't you *make* me do my homework?" he now wonders.

One son is incensed because too often I use my car at night and force him to make other arrangements, rather than handing over the keys.

My nine-year-old lectured me most of the week for being annoyed with his sister's antics. "She's only a baby, Mom. She's not trying to make you mad on purpose. I heard you tell a huge group of people that when Dad and I went to one of your talks. Remember? Isn't that what you say about babies?" This is not what a mother needs to hear on a day when she's not practicing what she preaches.

But then there are memories of brighter days. Like the afternoon Brian came in and said, "I heard you and Dad up with the baby last night. You must be tired. I'll make dinner."

Or the afternoon Sean did my car pool duties and said, "Why don't I take the baby? You look like you could use some solitude."

Or simple things like the Mother's Day card Thomas made. "I love you, Mom," he wrote carefully. "I'm glad you like my report card. Even if it was bad. I would still love you."

I looked at it and said, "Well, Tom, you need to know that even if it were bad, we would still love you."

With a huge grin he said, "Boy, Mom, you understand everything."

Life is not always as easy to understand as that card, but as he headed for the yard still grinning, I felt a warmth of maternal stirrings. Erin, our one-year-old wild child, had fallen asleep on my shoulder, snuggling close and smelling like baby powder, instead of bananas, for a change. It was a fine moment. It didn't last, of course. But just briefly there, I felt like a "natural-born mother."

Be a "Good Enough" Parent

When I was thirty I had more energy...or less sense. I remember embracing the new year enthusiastically, with long lists of resolutions, guaranteed to make me a better person in six weeks' time. "Lose twenty pounds by February first...or else!" I would write. "Never swear in front of the children again. Write to Mother once a week. Be patient. Be understanding." Etcetera, etcetera, etcetera.

The problem was, I was always disappointing myself. So I gave up on "never" and "always." Now sometimes I'm patient. Sometimes I'm moderate. And sometimes I swear.

The late Rudolf Dreikurs called on parents to "have the courage to be imperfect." Bruno Bettelheim refers to "good enough parenting." As parents, we all tend to be pretty hard on ourselves. It's too easy to focus on our mistakes rather than congratulate ourselves on our successes. I think a realistic approach to more effective parenting is an attempt to handle day-to-day problems with a fresh attitude now and then. The overall picture becomes brighter when we start adding up the little incidents we've handled well.

So from my frequent mistakes, my many successes, and my hopes for the new year, I've drawn up a moderate list of New Year Resolutions for parents:

One: Don't offer a choice to your child unless you really intend it to be one. For example, say, "Dinner will be ready soon," rather than, "Would you like some dinner soon?" if you expect her to sit down and eat.

Two: The next time your child does something really stupid or thoughtless, try to respond as you do when your best friend, spouse, or lover does something stupid or thoughtless.

Three: When your child comes home from a party or the movies and has a terrible stomachache...before you begin the lecture on popcorn, soda, and "I told you so," pause and remember how much you appreciated it the last time you overindulged and your friend, spouse, or lover responded, "I told you not to go for that last plate of nachos..."

Four: The next time your boss makes unreasonable demands on your time, say "no" as quickly as you would if your child tried to make unreasonable demands on your time. Then go home and play Monopoly with your ten-year-old.

Five: If your daughter wants you to play a video game and you dread the thought of it, tell her so. But find something you can both enjoy and do that instead. What she really wants is some time with you.

Six: The next time your son calls from school with an SOS because he left his report on his desk at home, instead of thinking about the effort he put in and racing to school with the paper, think about the importance of life skills. Remember, we can't learn from our mistakes if parents save us from making any!

Seven: Don't provide your child with so many activities or opportunities that she never has time to stare at the patterns raindrops make as they fall against the window, or watch a robin build a nest, or listen to herself think. (Children learn by example...we all need to do more of this!)

Eight: Remember the five-year-old's definition of a sweater: "It's what my mother makes me wear when she's cold." Then, after providing the boots, hats, and mittens, let your offspring take responsibility for their own comfort.

Nine: Spend some time now and again thinking about (or even writing about) your own childhood, the memories good and bad. Remember how you hated it when your mother said, "...and wipe that look off your face"? Have you heard yourself directing that at your own child? Why? What could you say or do instead? Remember how you loved it when your mother interrupted an important activity of her own to join you in something important to you? Have you done that this week? This month?

Ten: Hug your child for no reason at all on a regular basis. When we say, "I love you," or "I'm proud of you," right after our child has helped us out or done well at a task, it is easy for her to make the erroneous assumption that our caring is dependent upon her performance. Often the hug is most needed when she's just broken a neighbor's window, or flunked a spelling test, or helped herself to the pie we just made for a friend in need.

At our house the democratic process is really valued. Children, as well as adults, practice freedom of speech. My son Brian just edited these resolutions and proclaimed with enthusiasm, "You know, Mom, you sure know what it takes to be a great parent....If you would only get in the habit of following your own advice!"

Kids—Like Parents—Just Aren't Perfect

Lately I've been resenting the fact that there are still daily reruns of "The Brady Bunch." It all started when I sat sharing a cup of coffee with a teary-eyed friend whose son had recently been lying about taking money from her bureau. She questioned causes between sobs. "Maybe I work too many hours...maybe if I weren't divorced," and so on.

"I know it's hard," I tried to console, "but kids do these things on the way to growing up."

Later, visiting with another friend, we talked seriously about our adolescent sons: hers thrown off the school bus for harassing another student, mine suspended for inappropriate behavior in the school halls. "It's so hard," my friend confided. "Yet I always think it's harder somehow because we are a stepfamily."

I returned home to find my spouse fuming because yet another of our teenage offspring had lied in regard to his whereabouts. When we questioned him about his motives, he responded, "I really wanted to go badly and I knew you wouldn't let me. I thought you were being unfair and I knew I'd be safe, so I lied so I could be with my friend. I thought you wouldn't find out." Though we were upset and enforced some limits on our son's freedom as a result of the incident, we found ourselves consoling each other with the fact that our son's explanation was similar to what too many of us give when we bend rules for our own purposes.

Many of us find ourselves running late and drive to work above the speed limit with an eye on the rearview mirror. Like our youngsters, we count on not getting caught. Or we slip our six-year-old into the amusement park as "under six," or our thirteen-year-old into the movies as "twelve and under." We decide that the exorbitant rates are unfair; thus we are acting in a way that doesn't jeopardize our integrity. The system is wrong; the rules are wrong; we are right.

Yet when our children test limits or break rules, we often dive into a pool of self-doubt, guilt, and frustration. We question our marital status, our family makeup, or our level of job involvement, instead of accepting that kids, like parents, are just not perfect.

We are worthwhile and of value to our youngsters even when we err in our parenting efforts. We can strive to nurture the courage to allow imperfection in our children. It is important for youngsters to feel they are worthwhile even when they make mistakes.

This doesn't mean overlooking unacceptable behavior. Children need to understand and deal with the consequences of their actions. They need to discuss reasons for rules within the family system. But they also need support from parents as they learn to deal with their mistakes or lack of judgment. This is difficult for us as parents. We frequently judge ourselves and our children too harshly.

Only on "The Brady Bunch" is the most serious transgression of the teenage years stealing the mascot from the rival school's team. In real life, we have to deal with experimentation with alcohol and drugs, with academic and social problems, with lies and disappointments. It is painfully difficult to be a teenager today, and sometimes painful to be a parent, also.

When the first big wave of adolescent difficulties hit at our house, we ran to the comfort of good friends who have raised two fine young adults. "What can we do?" we pleaded in distress.

"Absolutely nothing," our friends said encouragingly, "but wait for it to pass!" Just to make us feel better, they added, "You may not have to deal with disruptive behavior at school again, or maybe even lying, but it's probably time to decide which of the cars you care least about...nobody raises teenagers without a few dented fenders!"

If Parents Could Only Relax More...

I saw my friend Kay today. Being with her always puts me in a good mood. When we met sixteen years ago, I was pregnant and had an eighteen-month-old baby. She had a house full of children ranging from a preschooler to teenagers. We were both members of a group that met frequently to do crafts, talk about our children, drink coffee, or share an evening out.

In those days, Kay was terribly concerned about the length of her teenagers' hair, the quality of their schoolwork, and getting them to wear slacks, not jeans, to church. At the time, it seemed to me she was awfully upset about things that weren't so bad. Then in my early twenties, I sometimes wore jeans to church myself.

"Margaret is so adorable, Kay," I would sometimes say.

"Try living with her," Kay would respond, often through clenched teeth. Pompously, but privately, I vowed never to let my feelings for my own little darlings reach such a sad low.

Well, years have passed and my vow has been broken. I smile politely in the church basement when parents come over to applaud my son's efforts at baby-sitting. When I ask one of the boys to sit at home, the sighs can be heard from afar. "Again?" I hear, even if it's been weeks since their father and I went out for an evening.

"'Fourteen and forty equals disaster,'" my son Brian reads aloud from a book called *Bringing Up Parents*, which he has recently been reading. Sometimes I believe it. But Kay tells me I'll live through it. She is tanned; she looks relaxed and wonderful. The lines of worry that I recall from our early years are gone from her face. I know where they went. I saw them in the mirror this morning when I brushed my teeth.

Two nights ago, my seventeen-year-old son lost his car keys in the sand and called home, hoping for the second set to be delivered to Hampton Beach. We had just gotten ready for bed. Last night, he called from Dunkin' Donuts in Seabrook. The fan belt in his car had broken. Could we drive him and his friend to her house? She would bring him home later. We had just gotten ready for bed.

"Tonight," I told my friend Kay, "I'm watching the late show and staying dressed." Kay laughed sympathetically.

"You know what's great about being my age?" she asked. I could quickly think of a long list, but I waited for her response. "You only remember the good times and you can laugh about the things that seemed so difficult when you were going through them." She talked with enthusiasm about the whole family coming home for a clambake—an annual tradition. The siblings, who once could not share the same backseat of a car, couldn't wait to see each other. She laughed as she told me the stories that her children, now in their thirties, finally had the courage to tell her.

First, it was the story of the missing table leaf. For years at holiday times, her noisy household would fall silent when she would complain again that table leaves don't just disappear. A short time ago, they finally told her what had happened to the missing leaf: it was sawed in half to finish a backyard tree house; it was the only wood they could find! She told me that she had prided herself for years on the fact that her kids never snuck out of the house at night. Recently, the boys laughingly told her that that was true, but she would die if she knew how many friends had snuck in for the night without her knowing. She laughed heartily as she told her tales.

"If only we could relax more while going through the tough years," she told me. "We should all laugh more; not take things so seriously. If I had it to do over, I wouldn't get so upset at every little thing. I would see the minor transgressions as signs of healthy egos developing. The ones I feel sorry for are the perfect children of perfect parents who can't make a mistake or their sense of self crashes completely."

"It's a lot easier to think like that when they're raised, Kay," I said.

"But it's more important to think like that now," she responded.

"I'll give it a try," I concluded. I thought about that a lot as I drove home.

The teenage destination tonight is Canobie Lake—a lot farther than Hampton or Seabrook. "Did you fill your gas tank? Check the oil? Cash your check?"

He's walking out the door to avoid my litany. "I'm all set, Mom, *really!*" he shouts from the garage. "If there's a problem, I'll call."

"I bet you will," I mutter under my breath.

"What?" he shouts again.

"I said it looks like a great night for the roller coaster!" I shout enthusiastically. He smiles and waves as he backs out of the drive. I feel pleased with myself. I'll do this more often. No sharp answers. Besides, it couldn't happen three nights in a row. But I'm still staying up for the late show—just in case.

My Fashion Sense Is All Wet

Popular columnist Judith Viorst published a small, humorous volume many years ago entitled *It's Hard to Be Hip Over Thirty*. We purchased several copies to give as gifts as, one by one, our generation reached that age we once vowed never to trust. We offered the book, in good spirit, to our friends as we all became less hip with the passage of time.

As another decade has slipped away, we seem to be redefining the meaning of hip. For many of us, it is now what stands between us and feeling completely comfortable in swimwear as the summer descends. This point was rubbed in at my house the other day when I brought home the swimsuit I was planning to wear in public in the near future.

I bought a new suit because the one I chose last year created such negative feelings on the part of those around me that I couldn't face donning it again. When I took it out of the bag last spring, my oldest son said, "I thought you got a blouse for Nana for Mother's Day."

His brother added thoughtfully, "Besides, that doesn't look like it would fit. It's just her style, but it looks small."

Humbly, I informed them that the swimsuit was for me. "But, Mom," the two teenagers protested, "You're not that old—at least you could go for a popular color. Why make yourself look older than you are?"

Never mind that I have bitten my tongue as these two walk out in brightly flowered shorts and even brighter shirts that don't match; that I have welcomed their friends without raising an eyebrow at various degrees of spiked hair; that I even kept myself from staring at the dangling fishbone earring one young man wore...I mean, who am I to question individual tastes and styles?

So this year I was more careful. I looked in magazines. I checked predominant colors in the stores. I clung to my right to select a style appropriate to my age and activity level (running after a one-year-old), but tried to go for enough fashion that my sons would not be embarrassed to say hello if, by accident, we should occupy the same stretch of New Hampshire shore.

My trial run was a morning at the beach with my neighbor, who is always on top of the latest styles. "The suit is perfect for you," she said encouragingly. "Much better than last year's." So I was unprepared for another dismal response from the younger generation.

"The colors are super," said one son as I held up the suit when the boys got home.

"The style is really cute," said the next son, "but it will be years before she grows into it!" Suddenly it dawned on me—they thought the suit was for their little sister.

Oh, well, I guess that proves I'm finally thinking young. I just have difficulty reaching a balanced sense of fashion. Judith Viorst knew it years ago: It's hard to be hip over thirty!

Let's Congratulate Ourselves, Mothers of the World!

"Mother's Day Special," the sign in the window reads. Pink flowers surround the letters; vacuum cleaners surround the sign! At the card shop, doggerel verse abounds, filling cards with hearts and flowers and deep, gold letters: MOM. In another shop, aprons are on display. "Every Mother is a Working Mother," says one; next to it, "For this I spent four years in college?"

Restaurants, florists, and candy shops gear up for that Sunday in May when the nation pays tribute to mothers. Many moms will have a brief break from cooking and dishes. Then it's Monday, and the moms of the country return to their jobs, their housework, and their child rearing—largely without the support of society, their spouses, or each other.

To many, that probably sounds exaggerated or harsh. Though we talk about progress and change, current research indicates that working women still bear almost all the responsibility for housework. Though women employed outside the home do less housework than full-time homemakers, they still do the vast majority of what needs to be done for the home and the family.

The distribution of workload is similar in the realm of parenting. Though many working dads today are nurturant, involved fathers, it is most frequently mothers who know what size everyone wears, who has had which shots, and what the teachers' names are.

The cultural norms of a society go deep. Recently a colleague of mine, facing the end-of-semester paperwork all teachers dread in May, said, in jest, of course, "Every year at this time I think I'd love to just get married and stay home to raise kids!" The fact that we continue to make light comments in this manner, or use the word "just"—as in "just a housewife"—implies that we've all been conditioned to think the job requires no skills, is a shelter from the real world, or is easier than what the rest of us do in our place of work.

For those who have spent years of hard labor in this job of mother/home-maker, this consensus is a source of pain. These women know they are bright, articulate, and hardworking. They know they have things to say and contributions to make, and so they resent it when they find themselves looking at the back of someone's head after responding to an inquiry about their occupation with the words, "I'm home with a two-year-old."

"You almost feel guilty," one at-home mother recently confided to me. "Like you're too lazy to go out and do something interesting." There it is again, that implication that working with young children isn't important or interesting. I'm sure that Harvard's T. Berry Brazelton doesn't feel that way about his years of work with young children.

Parenting young children is important work; very real work. In fact, those mothers who do choose to stay home full time with their youngsters have such a deep commitment to homemaking and child rearing that they feel it's the only right way for a child to be raised. But that presents another problem. There is no one right way for the needs of growing children to be met. Many of us want and need to work outside the home, whether we have very young children or not. The majority of American women do work outside of the home.

It is often the feeling of these women that when someone says, "I really admire you. I don't know how you manage. I know I couldn't work all day and still be a good mother and homemaker!" that with the compliment comes the subtle insinuation that it probably can't be done; that children of working mothers suffer. Funny that society never makes comments about the suffering children of working fathers.

It's still pretty much hard times for mothers. The self-sacrificing mother of the fifties was replaced by the supermom of the eighties. Women have more choices now, but it's hard to find peace. Mothers at home focus on the increasing pressure to be part of the labor force. Working moms still feel the burden of wondering if they might be neglecting their offspring. We could use support from each other. We should judge less and encourage more. It's hard mothering, no matter what the circumstances are.

During one of the finer years of my life, I was in the privileged position of having a wonderful and loving full-time housekeeper and child care provider while I taught kindergarten and did full-time graduate work. Not only did this person love our children and manage our home in a more efficient way than we'd ever done, she left homemade soup on the stove for supper. For an entire year, we experienced only the joys of parenting, while someone else did the hard, time-consuming day-to-day tasks that living with young children involves. Meanwhile, everyone who knew me kept telling me I was amazing...teaching school and doing graduate work with three young children!

When the year was over and I was home full time but unaccustomed to the fatigue of homemaking and child-rearing duties, I was exhausted. Beyond that, there was no more paycheck. The stimulation of my colleagues in graduate school was not comparable to playing Chutes and Ladders or checkers. It was harder work than I'd done in a while. It was difficult to adjust. Yet invariably, whenever I ran into an acquaintance, his or her first comment was, "After that rigorous graduate program, it must feel great to be doing nothing!"

There's that basic assumption again. Perhaps it will be years before we rid the language of these attitudes; before we stop using the word "helping" to refer to a man doing his housework, or the word "baby-sitting" to refer to a father parenting his children.

In the meantime, let's congratulate ourselves, the mothers of the world. Those who work at home and those who work outside; the mothers who wipe noses and bottoms, the mothers who build houses and court cases. Let's celebrate mothers who fly airplanes and mothers who fly kites! Happy Mother's Day!

It Was Great, but It's Over Too Soon

Raising children, it seems to me, can be reasonably compared to riding a roller coaster: some haven't the stomach for it.

For those hooked on the experience, though, the thrill of it all is worth the ups and downs, the wondering if you can handle the next big dip. Some of us have been known to gag, on occasion, after a particularly harrowing round; yet, aware of this possibility, we are drawn back to ride again.

I remember the first time I rode a coaster. It was at Glen Echo in Washington, D.C. I remember staring up at it, hearing the screams of the riders. "Scared, aren't you?" my brother asked.

"Sure," I answered, "but I'm ready." I trembled as I waited in line. "What if I'm really not ready for this?" I wondered silently, while showing my bravado outwardly.

Many years later, pregnant with my first child, the waiting was just as agonizing. "What if I'm really not ready for this?" I asked myself. But, again, it was too late. The experience was there, pulling me along, ready or not.

The past eighteen years have been somewhat like the roller coaster rides of my life. Watching my son grow from a boy to a man has had its moments. Looking back, it's easy to highlight the major lows and highs, the agony and the ecstasy, as they say. For a while, it seemed he would never manage without training wheels.

There was the kid in fourth grade who wouldn't leave him alone. It ended in a bloody brawl on the steps outside the school. The teacher called and said, "Sean and Bobby had some blows—you'd better get down here right away. Sean is awfully upset." I feared he'd been taken apart, as his tormentor had been threatening to do for weeks. Heart pounding, I raced over and found Sean untouched but in tears as the teacher wiped blood from the face of his adversary. It seems he'd finally been pushed too far and had fought back. He was crying at the realization that he'd hurt someone enough to make him bleed.

The exhilaration that accompanies watching your child grow and pursue knowledge of the world around him makes up for being told that your political views are "sound but limited," your fashion is "dated," your music belongs in elevators.

Recently, a classmate of his took my groceries to the car at the supermarket and commented on his recollection of a "great" party we'd had for Sean when he was ten.

"You've got a good memory," I laughed.

"You always had good parties," he said.

I felt misty driving home, wondering if those brighter spots of childhood will balance the hard times for Sean: the friends who died too soon, leaving emptiness and confusion; the romances ending in heartbreak; the politicians who've lied and set a poor example; the times his parents screwed up. Why does it seem to me his boyhood has been filled with so many experiences that should have waited till later?

Yet he's made it. He's fine. It was a struggle getting from flunking algebra freshman year to making honor roll and acceptance at college, but he's made it. Despite my perception that the world of his youth is so much harder than the one I took on years ago, he seems capable, ready, able to handle it.

"I ordered Tracy's flowers for the prom," he told me yesterday. "A gardenia with peach-colored roses on either side to match her dress." He seems pleased; excited, even. "We're going in Bill's car," he goes on. "It's so much more spacious than mine. What with the gowns and all, it makes more sense." I talk with him a bit more about plans and after-prom activities, and then he says he should go up and study some physics before it's time to go to work.

Has it been only ten years since the third-grade teacher said he daydreamed too much? I wouldn't have worried so much then if I could have imagined the serious, responsible young man who just headed out the door. I feel so proud, so lucky.

My thoughts are jolted back to the present as the door bangs and Tom, my third-grader, walks in. "You oughta see Sean's bike," he shouts exuberantly. "It's got massive cobwebs all over it. He's never used it since he got his car."

A lump rises in my throat and I think of the training wheels again. Where did the time go? Cautiously, Tom changes the subject. "Mrs. Smith says my mind hasn't been enough on my work this week."

"Oh?" I ask. "What's it been on?"

"Oh, stuff," he says. "Fishing, my new bike, sleeping over at Sherm's house, and going to the Red Sox game. Are you mad?"

"I want you to get all of that phonics done before you leave for Sherm's," I say, striving for an I-mean-business tone of voice. But silently I'm thinking, it's okay. You're just a boy. What better thoughts for a spring day than fishing and a new bike? Childhood is brief. Savor it. Soon enough you'll have massive cobwebs on your bike and be off to the big world.

Graduation is just a few weeks away. Today Sean is busy writing out announcements to relatives. I remember my own feelings at his age: hesitant to let go of the familiarity of home and high school friends, yet eager for college and the world beyond my home town. Some things never change—like raising kids and riding roller coasters.

My mind returns to Glen Echo thirty years ago. The screaming is over, my heart is still pounding, but I've done it! I made it! I look at my brother somewhat smugly. "Let's go again," I say. "It was great—but it was over too soon."

As I said, raising kids and riding roller coasters are a lot alike. It was great, Sean, but it's over too soon. Happy graduation!

10

Child and Society

Batteries Not Included

It's begun already. In Saturday morning commercials, the Care Bears march across the screen singing "Jingle Bells" (to get you in the mood) and mention that you can enjoy their songs at your house for only $9.98 (tape) or $11.98 (compact disc)!

This sets the stage for the high pressure push of toys; toys that we have come to expect at this holiday time of year. Children are most vulnerable to these slick advertisements, which create unrealistic expectations destined to hurt—unless we have a plan to protect our youngsters from such exploitation.

What can parents do to combat the influence of television advertising? It isn't easy. Children's commercials cost advertisers more than five hundred million dollars annually. Without question, the smiling toy manufacturers reap the benefits, but at our expense and that of our children.

It is within the power of parents to tackle this problem, but it takes courage! First, we must take the time to watch television with our children, alerting them to the discrepancies we see and hear in commercials. Madison Avenue techniques transform poorly constructed, battery-operated plastics into toys guaranteed to thrill and delight every child. Phrases like "each item sold separately" or "batteries not included" elude these young consumers. These are the things which parents should point out to their children.

Plan a trip to the toy store. Often the size of a toy is grossly misrepresented on the screen. The child is expecting more than the toy has to offer. Frequently, children feel frustrated and disappointed. Not knowing the real source of their betrayal, they direct their rage at their parents, who also feel betrayed. Having purchased exactly what a child requested, parents are anticipating a response of delight, not depression! So let the children browse in the toy store. Encourage them to see and hold the actual item without the lights, camera, and action!

Children need to know what "battery operated" and "batteries not included" mean. They need to know that batteries go dead, and what replacement costs can amount to. Are they willing to spend their own allowance to keep toys "battery operating?"

Young children, influenced by television commercials, often have strong preferences about the exact toy they want. Comparable substitutes, lacking extensive television exposure, are often a disappointment. And it is difficult for parents to make a disappointing choice for their children at holiday time. However, it is questionable whether durable toys, demanding imaginative use, are more disappointing, in the long run, than that familiar, heavily-advertised toy that breaks before the holiday comes to an end.

Take the time to listen to your children, to watch and critique commercials together, and to visit the toy store for a first-hand look at that much coveted item. It can make the holidays more satisfying and pleasant for children and their parents.

Warning: These Toys R Us!

Across the street from the child care center, where war toys are not among the playthings, a murder has taken place. The director requests that police cover the body. "Not before the coroner arrives, lady," the officer replies. Parents, arriving with young children, are horrified. Five-year-old Anthony grabs a long, narrow block. Enthusiastically making machine gun noises, he runs through the room, pointing his block at several children.

The local news commentators are at the door. With little regard for the children inside, the anchorman pushes the director for a few minutes of her time. The director has refused entrance. As the cameraman films the outside of the center, the anchorman tries again. "All we want is a few responses from the children to this outburst of violence in our usually quiet community."

Young Anthony pauses by the director. He looks from the microphone in the anchorman's hand to the block in his own. Forcefully, he spits out his machine gun sounds. "You're dead," he says, and walks away. The anchorman probably didn't notice, but he'd just gotten his sound bite!

Tom Brokaw is interviewing the mayor of New Orleans. "Juvenile crime," the mayor states, "is destroying American cities. Kids and guns are our problem here." The same evening, Brokaw reports on the nightly news that the nation has seen its first "ride-by" shooting. Eight shots from an officer's gun stopped the thirteen-year-old, who fell from his bicycle as passers-by ran for shelter.

The question, "Should children play with toy guns?" has been raised frequently in the past thirty years. Prior to that, it was not much of an issue. Children played cowboys and Indians. Guns and holsters were a natural for gift giving. There was the Davy Crockett craze, which gave way to G.I. Joe. In the 1950s, our parents didn't ponder the impact of these toys. The issue began to draw serious attention in the sixties. Assassination, crime, and violence were becoming commonplace. The six o'clock news brought the horrors of Vietnam into every American living room. At that time, families were not as aware of the effects of TV on children. So while parents listened to the news, children watched and learned.

What does all of this have to do with children, toy guns, and aggression? Perhaps more than most parents want to accept. As violence continues to permeate American lives, some of the initial shock has begun to wane. I vividly remember the November day in 1963 when John F. Kennedy was shot. We were stunned and silent. Young children, unable to understand, were hushed in deference to adult reactions. I also remember my sons returning from school the day John Hinckley, Jr. shot at President Reagan. "Hey, Mom," they said in the same tone in which they reported a coming snowstorm, "Somebody tried to kill the president." These were not calloused youngsters. It's just that they know of shootings. People shoot at presidents, musicians, students, and the Pope.

The world watched as Los Angeles police officers battered Rodney King. Coverage of bombings at the World Trade Center or violence in Sarajevo came into the home with the local weather. Children privy to all this information will be affected by it. "How horrible to have your mom dead and think your own dad might have chopped her up," my eight-year-old daughter said calmly at the dinner table.

At the local Arts in the Park festival, a storyteller asked for the name of a famous person. "O.J. Simpson!" was shouted in unison by the four- to ten-year-olds in the audience. Amy Fisher came in second. Michael Jackson and Tonya Harding were the last of the celebrities the youngsters could remember.

Complacent acceptance of crime and violence is worrisome. How will this generation, which volunteers the infamous when asked about the famous, come of age? Where are the scientists, musicians, artists, and policy makers who should be our children's heroes?

A trip through the mall provides some insights. Power Rangers and Fred Flintstone, sporting his club, peer out at us from T-shirts, pajamas, backpacks, and action figures. Profit, not responsibility to our young, seems to be shaping our policies. There are moral issues involved in our blatant acceptance of the current trend focusing on crime and violence as a way of boosting sales and ratings. Despite the increasing debate over TV violence, a study recently released by the A.F. Guggenheim Foundation reports a 41 percent increase in violence on broadcast television over the last two years. The report includes the fact that news programs, not entertainment, show the sharpest rise in coverage of violence.

An increasing body of research shows that playing with toy guns prompts aggression and antisocial behavior, including kicking, fist fighting, pushing, shoving, damaging property, and threatening to hurt someone. Children associate guns with violence and their play then generalizes into other aggressive activity. Parents concerned about aggressive behavior and serious sibling spats need to rethink the war toy dilemma.

For a long time it was considered healthy for children to vent aggressive feelings through gun play. Current research challenges this concept. Acting out aggression, viewing it on TV, or seeing it in real life does not purge children of these feelings, but actually increases aggressive tendencies. Regardless of parental views on gun control or the purpose of real weapons in the real world, the knowledge we now have about children's aggression and violence demands some rethinking about the appropriateness of guns as playthings for children. So often parents rationalize, "We've never purchased a toy gun and our child still uses every stick, baseball bat, or ruler for a weapon. Does it really make a difference?" By forcing children to improvise, we lessen the impact of violent play. The child uses more energy imagining and less on the resultant aggressive behavior. More importantly, when we provide children with toy weapons, we are openly giving our approval to the behavior associated with guns: violence and hurting others.

Violence on the playground and after school are frequent topics of discussion these days. There are fights in the classroom and fights on the school bus. There are fights in the cafeteria and fights during basketball practice. Parents are afraid; they don't want their children bullied or victimized. Family support groups meet to discuss the problem. But working against any efforts to curb violence in our schools or society are those toy manufacturers and television producers who continue to offer the glories of war as desirable play. By refusing to purchase violent toys, T-shirts, lunch boxes, or sweatshirts, parents set a responsible example for their offspring. By monitoring family TV viewing, parents can make a difference. The facts are in. To offer children war toys and violent TV programming and be surprised by their aggressive behavior is like offering children candy and soft drinks and being shocked at cavities!

"I Don't Need This
at the End of the Day"

As families settle into autumn routines, with the children back in school, lots of moms who were home for the summer return to other jobs. This is also the time of year when many women reenter the workforce for the first time since joining the ranks of parenthood.

A routine these parents must get used to is what educator Ellen Galinsky calls the "arsenic hour." Those familiar with end-of-the-day scenes at day care will probably agree that Ms. Galinsky does not exaggerate.

It's often a difficult time for parents, children, and child care providers. A typical scene might involve a parent eagerly driving up to her child's center or day care home. Warm stirrings of love and anticipation fill her heart as she thinks of reuniting with her child after a long day's work. But instead of racing happily to Mom's open arms, the child runs the other way, shouting angrily, "You came too soon!" Or, even worse, hitting or kicking the bewildered parent.

Parental response ranges from sadness ("I was so looking forward to being with her—why does she do this?") to anger ("I don't need this at the end of the day!") to embarrassment ("What must it look like to the teachers, that she doesn't even seem happy to see me?").

What parents need to know is that experienced child care providers are used to this scenario and know that it in no way reflects poorly on the parent/child relationship. Young children, away from parents all day, store up anxiety, disappointment, or anger over ordinary happenings (a fallen block structure; a special friend absent today; a snack they didn't like). When parents arrive, the child is able to let down all barriers. Secure that their parents love them, no matter what, children reserve their worst behavior for those who love them best: Dad and Mom.

Another factor contributing to hard times at the end of the day is that both children and parents need to shift gears. That's not easy, especially for children. Often the only opportunity parents have to shift gears is in traffic jams on the way from work to day care. This doesn't set the stage for calm reunions.

Youngsters often don't know what to do when their parents arrive. Do they still have to do what providers say? Or are they now under their parents' care again? Parents and providers can ease some of the strain by clearly defining whose job it is to get the child to the door, arranging similar departure routines for most days, and assuring each other that this "arsenic hour" is not representative of either the parent/child relationship or the teacher/child relationship. Most child care experts agree that if push comes to shove, it should be the teacher's job to manage the challenge, since the child is still on her turf. But both parents and providers need to agree on this so the child knows what to expect from whom.

Experts also agree that humoring the child can sometimes help at the "arsenic hour"—not a bad approach. After all, it's a long day for everyone!

Have You Hugged
Your Child Care Provider Today?

I am in Chicago. With twenty thousand other early childhood educators, I am attending workshops and polishing the tools of my trade.

In New Hampshire, my daughter is throwing up. Lynn, her child care provider, is helping her through this crisis. Erin is not yet two, and her mom hasn't been away on business until now. "Mother guilt" flames in my heart. Maybe she's throwing up because I'm in Chicago? On day two, Thomas and Brian are also throwing up. "Good," I think in my faraway hotel room. It's the flu. They all have it. Erin is not dealing with severe separation anxiety. Only I am.

I think of Lynn with a combination of gratitude and jealousy. She is holding my baby over the sink and then kissing the boo-boos away. I am learning new things, drinking coffee with colleagues, and discussing the child care dilemma.

One of the things I say about myself is that I am a working mother. This is not how Lynn would describe herself. For many years, she has cared for other women's children while those mothers go out to assorted occupations in the "working world." Lynn plays games with the children, gently instills in them consideration for others, and gets involved in their lives. She may be on the job at 5 A.M. if a flight attendant has an early schedule. She sometimes stays past 5:30 P.M. if a teacher is delayed in a parent conference. Yet she does not think of herself as a working woman.

I am reminded of a time several years ago when our former child care provider, Yvonne, said to me, "Let me make you a cup of tea before I go. I just don't know how you manage all this teaching and studying while raising a family. I've never worked, you know, since I was married." While Yvonne cared for our family when I was in graduate school, she also kept house for us. It was the only period in our family history when each of us knew where his or her socks were, or the scissors, or a safety pin. Everything was in its place. Yvonne always had time to take a walk, play hide-and-seek, or build a snowman. She was the one who taught my oldest boys to play checkers. Yet she insisted she was not a working woman.

There is a tremendous double standard in the U.S. when it comes to children and families. We say, "as American as Mom and apple pie." Yet mothering—caring for the young—receives, in actuality, so little regard that many of those engaged in the effort, even some who do it for wages, claim they are not working women.

My teenagers frequently have been given a twenty-dollar bill for moving a piece of heavy furniture, or for spending an hour shoveling someone's sidewalk and driveway. A medium-sized lawn, cut in a half-hour with a power mower, is worth ten or fifteen dollars. Yet when it comes to baby-sitting, many of us are outraged if a teenager expects three or four dollars an hour. Granted, we may be upset when we write a fifty-dollar check to a plumber who has occupied himself for forty-five minutes in our home, or a check for eighteen dollars for a bakery cake when, if we'd had more time, we could have baked it ourselves. But we always pay it, because "that's what they get these days."

This is where the child care situation stands alone. There is a deep cultural expectation that caring for children is something women should do for almost nothing. But if we must be away from our children, we cannot expect someone else to fill in for "a little pocket money."

Obviously, a man or woman who makes minimum wage cannot pay someone else minimum wage to care for his or her child. Thus, legislation and specific policies to support both families and providers is necessary. But in small ways, each of us contributes to the problem by putting such little value, monetary or otherwise, on this work of caring for the young in our culture.

Ask yourself if you could afford to pay more for your child care than you are paying. If you can, give your child care worker a raise. If you're paying ceiling rates at a center with sliding fees, and you can afford more, donate books or equipment. If you are already doing all you can financially, say, "Thank you—I couldn't manage without the fine job you do in my absence."

When you come in from a long flight, a day in court, or any of those other tasks in the "working world," take time to tell your child's caregiver that you know she's tired, too. Caring for youngsters is demanding labor. Remind her or him what a vital task he or she performs in this position. It's time we all gave more attention to this very important work. Behind most successful working women stand other hard-working women: our child care providers. They need our support—financial and moral. They deserve our respect and gratitude.

Thank you, Yvonne. Thank you, Gloria. Thank you, Lynn. You are some of the hardest-working women I know.

...And That's the Way It Is

My daughter's third-grade teacher gives the children jobs to do each week. I am in favor of this, since too few American youngsters feel needed and responsible. Last week, though, my daughter ran into problems with her assignment as News Reporter. The teacher, quite appropriately, expects the children to understand the news and explain it in their own words. She expects it to be of a serious nature and also that it be nonviolent. She pushes the children to search for the good going on in the world around them.

On this particular day, there were three primary stories in the news. One involved the mother of the Speaker of the House reporting that her son had called the First Lady "a bitch." The next involved brutal murders at a women's health clinic. The last questioned the admissibility of previous spousal abuse as evidence in the O.J. Simpson trial.

"What can I do, Mommy?" my daughter asked in distress.

"You need to tell your teacher that none of the news today is appropriate for sharing in class. She will understand," I assured her as I bundled her up and headed for the bus stop.

After she left, I started thinking about all of this and remembering the news stories of my childhood. There was the celebration over Alaska and Hawaii joining the Union. There was Sputnik and talk of Americans being first to put a man on the moon. The Peace Corps was established to reach out to international neighbors, and Head Start brought books and breakfast to youngsters who might otherwise go without. Each night, my brothers, sisters, and I knew to be quiet when our parents were watching the news. We also knew we could talk and laugh again once Walter Cronkite said, "And that's the way it is."

And "the way it was" was quite different from the world of news my young daughter watches. In my youth, the adults were in charge and all the children knew it. Our parents might have made many mistakes, but they accepted the adult role of parent and made no apologies for it. Knowing that sometimes made us feel angry, but it also made us feel safe.

The cover of *Newsweek* recently displayed a young child wearing a dunce cap. Under it were the huge black letters "SHAME"—and then the question, "How do we bring back a sense of right and wrong?" According to the article, "Americans are fed up with everything from teen pregnancy to drunk driving." Subtitles asked, "Whatever happened to sin?" and claimed, "There should be a way to condemn behavior that is socially destructive."

Psychologist Penelope Leach has published a sobering volume entitled *Children First*. In it, she claims that "Society relies on childhood socialization to produce good citizens but keeps child-apprentices in a separate world from the adults they need to emulate. Instead of learning to do as adults do, children are expected to do as adults say. Discipline that is achieved by the exercise of power can never be as effective as self-discipline achieved through influence."

This is why the magazine article on "shame" concerns me so. It discussed harsher penalties for adolescents who get into trouble. It discussed the need for a realistic and well constructed conscience. But nowhere did it address *example* as a way to restore to our young a sense of right and wrong.

Come on, America! The wise of every nation and generation have always known the best approach for raising good citizens: take the time to talk to children about right and wrong. Then consistently engage in the behaviors we wish our youngsters to emulate. When our nation's leaders do illegal drugs and run for office anyway; when politicians call each other "bitch" and "fag" while children are listening; and when parents punish children for lying, then cheat on their taxes and on each other; we cannot be surprised when our young show no remorse at wrongdoing.

Unlike my daughter's homework, this is not current events. It is old news. Plato said it all, over two thousand years ago: "The best way to train the young is to train yourself at the same time; not to admonish them but to carry out your principles in practice."

...And that's the way it is!

Additional
Resources

Resources for Parents

Bettelheim, Bruno. *The Uses of Enchantment*. New York: Alfred A. Knopf, 1976.

Bettelheim, Bruno. *Good Enough Parenting*. New York: Alfred A. Knopf, 1987.

Brazelton, T. Berry. *Working and Caring*. Reading, MA: Addison-Wesley, 1985.

Brazelton, T. Berry. *Families: Crisis and Caring*. New York: Ballantine Books, 1989.

Calladine, Carole and Andrew. *Raising Brothers and Sisters Without Raising the Roof*. New York: Winston Press, 1979.

Calderon, Mary. The Family Book About Sexuality. New York: Harper & Row, 1989.

Canape, Charlene. *The Part-Time Solution*. New York: HarperCollins, 1990.

Coontz, Stephanie. *The Way We Never Were*. New York: HarperCollins, 1992.

Crosby, Faye J. *Juggling*. New York: The Free Press, 1991.

Curran, Dolores. *Stress and the Healthy Family*. New York: Harper & Row, 1985.

Elkind, David. *The Hurried Child*. Reading, MA: Addison-Wesley, 1981.

Elkind, David. *Ties That Stress*. Cambridge, MA: Harvard University Press, 1994.

Hymes, James. *The Child Under Six*. 2nd Edition. West Greenwich, RI: Consortium Publishing Co., 1994.

Kelly, Marguerite and Elia Parsons. *The Mother's Almanac*. Revised Edition. New York: Doubleday & Co., 1992.

Kenniston, Kenneth. *All Our Children: The American Family Under Pressure*. New York: Harcourt Brace Jovanovich, 1977.

Lansky, Vicki. *Divorce Book for Parents*. New York: Penguin Books, 1989.

Leach, Penelope. *Children First*. New York: Alfred A. Knopf, 1994.

Lebowitz, Fran. *Social Studies*. New York: Random House, 1991.

McCracken, Janet Brown, Editor. *Reducing Stress in Children's Lives*. Washington, DC: National Association for the Education of Young Children, 1986.

Miller, Alice. *For Your Own Good: Hidden Cruelty in Child Rearing*. New York: Farrar, Straus, & Giroux, 1984.

Miller, Alice. *Thou Shalt Not Be Aware: Society's Betrayal of the Child*. New York: A Meridian Book, New American Library, 1986.

The Pleasure of Their Company. Prepared by the Bank Street College of Education. New York: 1981.

Rogers, Fred. *Mister Rogers' How Families Grow*. New York: Berkley Books, 1988.

Runyon, Beverly Browning. *The Overloving Parent*. Dallas, TX: Taylor Publishing Co., 1992.

Schor, Juliet B. *The Overworked American*. New York: HarperCollins, 1992.

Roiphe, Anne and Herman. *Your Child's Mind*. New York: St. Martin's Press, 1985.

Turecki, Stanley. *The Difficult Child*. New York: Bantam, 1985.

Wallerstein, Judith S. and Sandra Blakeslee. *Second Chances*. New York: Ticknor & Fields, 1990.

Resources for Children

Boegehold, Betty. *Daddy Doesn't Live Here Anymore*. New York: Western Publishing Co., 1985.

Boyd, Levy. *The Not So Wicked Stepmother*. New York: Puffin Books, 1989.

Crary, Elizabeth. *Mommy, Don't Go*. Seattle, WA: Parenting Press, 1986.

Hazen, Barbara Shook. *Why Can't You Stay Home With Me?* New York: Western Publishing Co., 1986.

Hitte, Katheryn. *Boy, Was I Mad*. New York: Parents Magazine Press, 1969.

Paris, Lena. *Mom is Single*. Chicago: Children's Press, 1980.

Rogers, Fred. *Going to Day Care*. New York: G.P. Putnam's Sons, 1985.

Stanek, Muriel. *All Alone After School*. Niles, IL: Albert Whitman & Co., 1985.

Seuling, Barbara. *What Kind of Family Is This?* New York: Western Publishing Co., 1985.

Stein, Sara Bonnett. *On Divorce*. New York: Walker & Co., 1984.

Vigna, Judith. *She's Not My Real Mother*. Chicago: Albert Whitman & Co., 1980.

Vigna, Judith. *Daddy's New Baby*. Niles, IL: Albert Whitman & Co., 1982.